Vienna – Impressions of a Dream City

VIENNA

Impressions of a Dream City

Hans Wiesenhofer (Photography)
Berta Sarne (Text)

Translated by Andrew Smith

Verlag Anton Schroll & Co · Vienna and Munich

© 1986 – Verlag Anton Schroll & Co, Vienna and Munich
All rights reserved: no part of this book, either text or pictures, may be reproduced in any form
Printed in Austria
Produced by: Agens-Werk Geyer + Reisser, Vienna
ISBN 3-7031-0626-3

Vienna, you will always be the city of my dreams for me . . . – runs a well-known sentimental Viennese song filled with a particular charm of its own, a tender, heartfelt, devoted declaration of the love which the Viennese feel for their city. Vienna – the city of many dreams! The poet Ladislaus Pyrker, patriarch of Venice, once even sang the praises of Vienna as "the foremost place in the world" – words which he wrote in the year 1822. – And today? Are they still at all valid more than one and a half centuries later?

However much the city may have changed, the Vienna of today has lost none of its charm. When we look for the delights, the special attractions which Vienna and Vienna alone has to offer, for its unique features or even trivialities, for its treasures and sensations, we are confronted with a rich variety of experiences, impressions and wonders.

Sometimes Vienna's special attractions are off the beaten track – delightful surprises meet you as you stroll through the streets and alleyways of the old city on the search for hidden treasures. However, it is not just the experience of charming façades, oriels, gateways and peaceful courtyards, or the multitude of medieval, baroque or Biedermeier houses and palaces which still survive. The astonishing thing for an observer with an open mind to history is the discovery that he has suddenly become aware of the continuity of history – and his walk becomes a journey back to a time in which he encounters the Vienna which was once the capital of a large empire.

This journey takes one even further back into the past, as the observer can trace the origins of the city with ease. Even today, you can still follow the outlines of the first walls of the "Castrum Vindobona" which the Romans founded in the first century AD as a border city and fortification.

The beginning of half a millennium of Roman rule is linked with the name of the great Roman emperor Marcus Aurelius. It was in Vindobona that this philosopher on the imperial throne wrote a part of his intellectual "self contemplations", and he also died here. Vindobona did not go under despite all the storms and confusion of the migration of nations, and many great figures in world history came on the scene here.

Vienna, first mentioned under the name of "Wenia" in the Salzburg annals of 881, was always a protective bastion and place of refuge or a hotly disputed garrison town. Ever since the 13th century, after the noble Babenberg family died out and the House of Habsburg entered the history of Austria, Vienna rose to become an international metropolis, always helping to shape the fate of Europe.

Thus the origins of this city lie in an area which corresponds to its subsequent importance. The Roman fortification was established at a site favoured by nature: at the centre of the Danube basin and at the point where the amber road running from North to South crossed the Danube.

This important point of intersection of vital ancient traffic routes determined a location more favourable than that of any other city on the continent: a location at the heart of Europe, but nevertheless immediately on the border with the East, and destined by fate to permanent confrontation with the East.

On a walk through the old city we can still trace out the course of the walls of the Roman fortress, which today corresponds to the streets Salzgries, Tiefer Graben, Naglergasse–Graben, Kramergasse–Rotgasse.

History shows that the city developed outwards from the centre, growing in concentric circles. The original nucleus was Roman and served for a long time – also serving as a refuge in the turbulent times of the migration of nations.

Vienna experienced a political and cultural upswing during the rule of the Babenbergs (976–1246). Duke Heinrich II Jasomirgott (1141–1177) moved his court from neighbouring Klosterneuburg to Vienna, and developed the city over an area similar to that of the former Roman settlement. This decision was to prove very important for the history of the city. It made Vienna the centre of the "Ostreich", and its growing importance was documented in the granting of a city charter and staple rights in the year 1221. This trade monopoly resulted in great economic prosperity. And at the same time the arts also flourished, and Walther von der Vogelweide, the most famous German lyric poet of the Middle Ages, celebrated "the delightful court at Vienna". Within the space of a few decades, the Babenberg capital reached about the extent of the present inner city. The fortifications erected at the time under Duke Leopold V – said to have been financed in part by the ransom money paid for Richard the Lionheart – enclosed the city until well into the 19th century. It was only Emperor Franz Joseph I who ordered them to be razed to the ground.

The civil populace lived within this ring of walls from the Gothic era to the Renaissance, and from the baroque age till the 19th century. The historical development of the city is reflected principally in its buildings. The wealth of architectural beauty that has been preserved will have to make up for what has been lost. Wars and building booms have destroyed much for ever, but even this is not completely lost. Much of the glamour of ancient palaces, churches and town houses has fortunately been saved for us in paintings, engravings and photographs which bear witness to changing times and styles, to the gradual growth of the city to this day – and all that has been lost has become history.

The brilliant painter Rudolf von Alt – foremost of the Viennese landscape painters of the Biedermeier age and the late 19th century – has bequeathed to us in his delightful watercolours what was left of old Vienna in his lifetime. There are also numerous engravers and lesser known landscape painters, and even amateurs, who with loving attention to detail and great precision, have immortalised idyllic squares, streets and alley-ways in their drawings.

Vienna had to survive two trials of strength as a mighty bulwark against the East, as a bastion of Christianity. For centuries the Turks had aimed at the conquest of Europe, and in 1529 and 1683 they reached the city of Vienna. The city withstood both sieges heroically with great sacrifice, thus proving its value as a fortification. Europe was freed of a threat that had existed for two and a half centuries. However, the struggle against the tenfold superiority of the Turks in the year 1683 could only be brought to a victorious conclusion at the last minute with the aid of a relieving army commanded by the King of Poland Jan Sobieski and Duke Charles of Lorraine.

Prince Eugene of Savoy also made a decisive contribution towards the victory. It was also he who finally banished the threat from the East with his military successes in the wars against the Turks in the Balkans. After the victory against the Turks, Vienna moved into the limelight of

European politics and was no longer a mere border stronghold. A new feeling of elation spread, stimulating architecture, the fine arts and music. Thanks to the genius of great architects, Vienna blossomed into a magnificent baroque metropolis. The men mainly responsible were Johann Bernhard Fischer von Erlach and Johann Lukas von Hildebrandt.

The suburbs encircling old Vienna, the result of centuries of organic growth, surrounded the nucleus of the city. In the year 1683, during the second siege by the Turks, this ring of beautiful villas and suburban houses and gardens was destroyed, burnt down and demolished so as not to give the Turks a foothold. Thus there was ample space and building ground which was safeguarded and protected by the new defensive wall of 1704.

There was now a surge of building activity, and an astonishing number of magnificent palaces shot up around the city. Within the space of a few decades, a sudden change also took place within the inner city: the narrow, high gabled Gothic houses gave way to wide fronted houses and palaces in which art and music were cultivated.

Where simplicity and unpretentiousness once ruled, there was luxury and magnificence.

The palaces had spacious stairways, the stairs of which were so wide that two crinolines could comfortably sweep down beside one another, and the steps so low that the ladies in their bouncing skirts seemed not to walk, but to float. A magnificent wrought iron park gate, behind which a palace can be made out distant and dreamy in the dusky haze brings to mind fabulous garden parties.

The memories and references to a great past hang as gilded plates and flagged house signs everywhere in the old city. They are at once cheerful and depressing, like messengers from another world, from the world of an imperial and aristocratic past.

Among the large number of baroque palaces in Vienna – of which there are about thirty in the inner city alone – there are two majestic buildings which must be mentioned as the most outstanding achievements of this era. They are an absolute must on the programme of any visitor to Vienna: Belvedere Palace and Schönbrunn Palace.

The builder of the Belvedere was that much praised "noble knight" Prince Eugene of Savoy, born in Paris in 1663 as the fifth son of Duke Eugene Moritz of Savoy, a brilliant general and statesman. He came to Austria in 1683 after – the irony of fate – Louis XIV had declared him unfit for military service. In the Austrian army he rapidly advanced to commander-in-chief, and in 1693 was appointed field marshall of the imperial troops. Not only did he develop his strategic abilities under three emperors – Leopold I, Joseph I and Karl VI – he was also a great patron of art and a scholar, the owner of a magnificent library and a priceless collection of copperplate engravings.

Prince Eugene associated with the greatest minds of his time, including Leibniz, Montesquieu and Voltaire. He summoned the poet Jean-Baptiste Rousseau to Vienna as a librarian. A man with a highly cultivated mind and of noble character, Prince Eugene must be regarded as a brilliant exponent of the baroque age. It is therefore understandable that his Palais Belvedere was the much admired cultural centre of Vienna. The glamorous celebrations which were held in the palace and park soon acquired a world-wide reputation, particularly as the prince was familiar with the imperial court in his capacity as adviser to Karl VI. A trait of character typical of the prince is revealed by the fact that he rejected Czar Peter the Great's offer of the crown of Poland.

Prince Eugene died in April 1736 in his Vienna town palace in Himmelpfortgasse and was buried in the Chapel of the Cross in St. Stephan's Cathedral.

The Belvedere – a mirror of the prince's work and many-sided interests and a monument to his great personality – can look back on an eventful history: as a palace full of celebrations and joie de vivre, but also a scene of farewells, never to return. It was here that Empress Maria Theresa gave a sumptuous farewell celebration for her beloved youngest daughter Marie-Antoinette on the occasion of her marriage to the dauphin. More than six thousand guests were invited to a masked ball with festive illuminations. The festivities were attended not only by the aristocracy, diplomats, university professors, civil servants and officers, but also by respected merchants and citizens with their families. Even the curious townsfolk could enter through the marble hall of the lower palace in the park in order to marvel at the illuminations. Everybody was permitted to share the joy in the honourable marriage of the empress's daughter, which was to tighten Austria's political bonds with France. Both palace and park were decked out in the fabulous glamour of baroque festive decorations and illuminations, filled with the cheerful joie de vivre of an era the end of which was already in sight. But at the time none of the merry dancers or admiring onlookers can have guessed that the delightful young bride was on her way to the guillotine.

The baroque pleasure in spectacles lived on in the public festivals in the park of Belvedere Palace during the Biedermeier era. The water fireworks of Anton Stuwer were extremely popular because – like Ferdinand Raimund's extravaganzas – they preserved the heroic gods of the baroque era as Biedermeier fairy-tales and catered for the delight of the Viennese in great pomp and pageantry.

Even the Lilac Festival and the Rainbow Festival, charity events organised by Princess Pauline Metternich in the spring of each year towards the end of the 19th century, attracted many Viennese. With plenty of food and drink, music and dancing, the Viennese liked to marvel at the illumination of the palace and the fireworks.

In 1894 Archduke Franz Ferdinand chose Belvedere Palace as his residence, and it was here that he prepared plans and reforms for his coming accession to the throne, and that he established his "counter court" to Schönbrunn, from which the ageing Emperor Franz Joseph I ruled. And it was from here that he set out for Sarajevo in 1914 – to meet his death from the assassin's bullets.

It was only in 1955 that a happier day dawned on this fairy-tale palace, when the State Treaty between Austria and the occupying powers was signed in the marble hall of the Upper Belvedere. On 15th May the red-white-red flag fluttered from the balcony of the palace as a symbol of liberty and independence regained, welcomed by a jubilant crowd of people.

And on mild summer evenings, anybody who feels so inclined can listen to the history of the palace during the "son et lumière", a dramatised light show. The narrative is spoken by prominent actors on tape, while spotlights immerse the parts of the palace referred to in changing colours.

Schönbrunn Palace takes us back to the time of Empress Maria Theresa. Only 23 years old when she succeeded Emperor Karl VI as Archduchess of Austria and Queen of Hungary and Bohemia after the death of her father in 1740, Maria Theresa was perhaps the most outstanding member of the Habsburg family. She defended her heritage with courage, tenacity and a great deal of political skill against half of Europe, and in particular against Friedrich II of Prussia. In 1745 she secured the crown of the Holy Roman Empire for her husband and co-regent Franz Stephan of Lorraine.

Despite all the challenges of foreign policy, Maria Theresa devoted herself resolutely to internal reforms, favouring economic and industrial development, introducing compulsory education, founding social institutions and, with the centralisation of the administration of the state in the "Theresian chancellery", laid the foundations for modern administration and bureaucracy.

She enjoyed tremendous popularity and won the love of her subjects as the "Mater Patriae" of her multilingual empire. Her remark "Better a moderate peace than a glorious war" is imbued with warmth and inspired by a respect for life.

Maria Theresa was an astonishing woman who achieved an admirable balance between her often difficult duties of state and her family life. She gave birth to sixteen children, for whom she was always an understanding mother. This is shown by her abundant correspondence, which also gives us extremely interesting cultural and historical insight.

In spite of her government duties and family obligations, the empress took a keen interest in the arts: she had Schönbrunn extended as her imperial summer residence, promoted music and theatre and even found time to enjoy herself at the masked balls which were so popular at the time.

After the sudden death of her husband in 1765, Maria Theresa never again ceased to wear mourning. The empress herself died in Vienna in November 1780 and was buried in a splendid sarcophagus in the crypt of the Capuchin Church. During her lifetime she had extended the time-honoured burial place of the Habsburgs and commissioned a magnificent double sarcophagus by Balthasar Moll. This sarcophagus exemplifies the baroque attitude to life, with its tremendous tensions between love of life, sensual pleasure and predilection for pomp on the one hand, and on the other a knowledge of the transience of everything mortal.

Joseph II – another member of the House of Habsburg to whom the Viennese opened their hearts – succeeded his mother to the throne in 1780. His reforms, inspired by the spirit of enlightenment, have gone down in history under the name of "Josephinism". One of his first acts as supreme head of state was the promulgation in 1781 of a tolerance patent which gave Protestants and Orthodox Christians freedom of religion. He also worked to improve the legal status of the Jews.

In many respects Joseph II proved to be an autocratic benefactor: he liberated the peasants from serfdom, abolished torture and in 1784 founded the "General Hospital" in Vienna. He also continued the educational and administrative reforms of his mother with great radicalism and resolution.

His liberal attitude to equality and efforts to be popular with his subjects are attested to by many anecdotes. When the aristocracy protested against the opening of the Augarten Park to the Viennese public, and suggested that the emperor might revise his decision, as people sometimes preferred to be "among their peers", the monarch is reputed to have replied: "Gentlemen, if I always wanted to remain among my peers, I should be able to walk only in the crypt of the Capuchin Church".

The emperor reduced the power of the Church by dissolving the monasteries and confiscating the lands of the religious orders and abbeys. Although his church laws allowed a division of dioceses and parishes which has remained to this day, they also dramatically restricted the colourful formalities, customs and rites of popular baroque religion. His enthusiasm for reform was considered excessive, with the result that many of his decrees had to be revoked. At all events, this revolution from the top down, the ten years of restless, almost revolutionary activity of his rule saved Austria from a revolution from the bottom up – at least until the year 1848. This was the year in which Vienna's revolutionary citizens and students gathered around the monument to Joseph II in front of the National Library. The equestrian statue showing the reformist emperor in the costume and pose of the Roman imperator Marc Aurel had become a symbol of the free spirit which they were demanding for the Habsburg nations. Their hopes were not to be fulfilled: the revolution was put down, and the old order of absolutism dominated the decades that followed.

The period of the Congress of Vienna was a highlight in the history of Vienna in more ways than one. The Napoleonic Wars had ended with the Battle of the Nations near Leipzig, and Napoleon had been banished to St. Helena. The Danube metropolis stood at the centre of European politics – for the last time, as events would show – as kings, princes and diplomats gathered to deliberate a new order for Europe. The host, Emperor Franz I, was once again one of the mightiest European monarchs, and the whole city celebrated the fact with him with all conceivable pomp and circumstance. Day after day, a variety of extravagant festivities was arranged, such as balls, carousels, hunts, masked balls, concerts and military parades. Prince de Ligne was moved to coin his famous quip "The congress dances, but does not progress". The manifold amusements seem to have occupied the illustrious guests more than politics, as contemporary historians have recorded. Originally scheduled for a couple of months, the congress went on and on. Once again, the magnificence of rococo and Empire were experienced here, like a gigantic firework display.

After the Congress of Vienna, the fate of Austria, and with it that of Europe, was securely in the hands of Clemens Prince Metternich for almost half a century. The bureaucracy developed under Maria Theresa functioned admirably, and even up until the 20th century, numerous aristocrats gave it a typically cosmopolitan character.

The personality of Metternich and his historic significance have been variously interpreted. As an uncompromising champion of the principle of monarchy, his political thinking was aimed strictly at maintaining the existing order. His reactionary police measures nipped any political activity in the bud and made it impossible to take steps to improve social grievances and injustices. The people of the city withdrew in helpless resignation to a modest life in a world of their own, to the idyll of Biedermeier civilisation. Metternich became a hated symbol of oppression and servitude, until he was eventually forced to resign and flee abroad by the March Revolution which broke out in 1848.

Sociability and love of beauty prevailed during the Biedermeier period, and a passion for the theatre also developed. Mozart's "Magic Flute" had its première at Emanuel Schikaneder's Theater auf der Wieden, and Beethoven's "Fidelio" was first performed at the Theater an der Wien, which has lost nothing of its popularity to this day. It was here, too, that the young Grillparzer first attained fame with his play "The Ancestress". People took pleasure in the romantic popular comedies of Ferdinand Raimund and in the comedies and critical social satires of Johann Nestroy. The bubbling humour and sparkling irony of their works enliven theatres both large and small to this day. And Fanny Elssler danced: she emerged from the musical world of Biedermeier Vienna just like all the great performers who still populate Vienna's musical firmament today.

And the musical genius of Strauss and Lanner sprang from the age-old love of the Viennese for violin playing, for music making – it was simply there and made music. Johann Strauss possessed the divine spark which has not gone out to this day. Thus it is that his masterpiece, the operetta "Die Fledermaus", is still performed by the Vienna State Opera.

According to the well-known Viennese literary man Hans Weigel, "Die Fledermaus" is a brilliant self-portrait of the city, and a key to the Viennese character can be found in the music and text of the operetta, both of which are equally appropriate: "Happy the man who can forget the things he is unable to change . . ." The French composer Jules Massenet said of Johann Strauss, that restive genius possessed by music, that he was the perfume of Viennese music.

Among the great figures in the musical life of Vienna in the early 19th century was Franz Schubert, whose talent was first recognised and furthered by accomplished amateur Viennese musicians. Pictures and engravings tell of the musical soirées and amateur music performances in the society around Franz Schubert, the same society which gave him encouragement and made it possible for him to reach an audience and find a publisher. His friends and patrons included the young Baron von Spaun and Franz von Schober, the painter Moritz von Schwind, the lyric poet Johann Mayrhofer, the poet and doctor Baron von Feuchtersleben and many others besides. And to this day, Viennese audiences love their "adopted" musical geniuses Haydn, Mozart and Beethoven and the Vienna-born Johann Strauss Father and Son, Franz Schubert and many of their contemporaries who gave the world a wealth of lovely melodies, and whose fame is immortal.

Apart from the Gothic and baroque epochs, the era which had the most decisive effect on the architecture of Vienna was the historicism of the Ringstrasse era. The idyll of the Biedermeier age changed to extroversion: the Ring, which encloses the inner city like a giant polygon, became a "magnificent architectural fancy dress", as Otto F. Beer appropriately described it.

Here the architect was able to realise his dream of a total work of art, instrumenting in styles instead of keys and combining them into a whole like a symphony.

When almost a decade had elapsed since the commotion of the March Revolution and the economic prosperity of the industrial expansion in Germany had also spread to the Habsburg empire, the young Emperor Franz Joseph I issued his famous "Autograph of His Majesty" to his minister of the interior Baron von Bach ordering him to extend the inner city by razing the ramparts together with ditches and fortifications, and to ensure thereby the "regulation and enhancement" of the residence and imperial capital.

An enormous complex of walls had to be razed in Vienna along with the adjacent rows of houses. A ring of fortifications some four kilometres in length was dynamited, and for decades a gigantic building site surrounded the inner city. The demolition of the walls and bastions had its opponents, particularly in strategic circles. They believed in Vienna's thousand-year destiny as a bulwark of the empire, and were unable to imagine an unfortified city.

In September 1859 the emperor approved the final draft that had been prepared from the proposals of Ludwig Förster, Eduard van der Nüll, August von Siccardsburg, Friedrich Stache and other architects: a magnificent boulevard with a width of 57 metres was to be laid out as a pulsating thoroughfare between the old city and the suburbs. The art historian Gustav Künstler wrote "This unique street does not lie in any particular part of Vienna, but has become an independent link between the centre and the surrounding districts, belonging equally to all, but not completely integrated with any".

That which took the place of the demolished bastions, walls and gateways was so outrageously new and magnificent that the sensitive citizen felt oppressed in the old city. However, many delightful fragments of old Vienna were preserved at the edge of the inner city, above which a wisp of the past still hangs. Opposite the university, at Mölkerbastei 8, is the Pasqualati house, where Beethoven rented a flat on the fourth floor several times in the years 1804–1815. He liked the unobstructed view to the slopes of the Vienna Woods, and it was here that he wrote his opera "Fidelio". Another genuine Biedermeier residence is the attractive house at Schreyvogelgasse 10, which has gone down in the chronicles of old Vienna under the legendary name of "Three Maidens House".

From an architectural point of view, the Ringstrasse is a total work of art, though for a long time various stylistic details were questioned. But the situation has long since changed, for today it is not only one of the greatest town planning achievements in Europe, but criticism of the architectural styles of the buildings has also subsided with the growing appreciation of historicism today. And the felicitous designation "Ringstrasse style" does justice to all the variety.

Gustav Künstler sees a deeper meaning in the adoption of various styles from other eras: "The democratic principle of parliamentarism appears in the attire of the ancient classical democracy, in Hellenic form (house of parliament); the meeting place of civic life takes its form from the heyday of the German middle classes in the late Middle Ages (Gothic town hall); and finally the seat of the sciences draws its shape from the cradle of the humanistic educational ideal, the Italian Renaissance (university)."

Along the Ringstrasse magnificent public buildings – the new Hofburg, the State Opera, the museums, the parliament buildings, the Burg

Theatre, the university, the town hall, the stock exchange and the law courts, to name but a few – stand side by side with the town houses of wealthy citizens. These sumptuous town houses designed by highly esteemed architects were a welcome means of expressing the need for grandeur of a new moneyed aristocracy – bankers and industrialists who had grown rich during this period of economic prosperity.

The urban expansion also made room for splendid monuments, and statues of generals, statesmen and artists were erected in parks and squares.

In 1873, the year of the World Fair in Vienna, when over seven million visitors flocked to the Danube metropolis, the Ringstrasse became the focal point of an international meeting-place. Particularly the section of the Ring between Kärntner Strasse and Schwarzenbergplatz, beginning with the then famous "Sirk Corner" with its fashionable café, soon became the centre of attraction for high society. In our century the former promenade of elegant society has fallen victim to the rushing motor car. But today the wonderful idea of the pedestrian precinct – already realised in parts of the inner city – meets the growing need for communication, thus improving the quality of life in the city.

The crowning of the Ringstrasse, the fulfilment of its purpose, as it were, was the procession to commemorate the silver wedding anniversary of the imperial couple on 28th April 1879. The painter Hans Makart, acclaimed as "king" of the Ringstrasse era, arranged this triumphal parade with groups of figures in historic costumes and led it himself, dressed in a black velvet costume and riding a white horse. In front of the outer palace gate the architect Otto Wagner had erected a marquee for Emperor Franz Joseph and Empress Elisabeth, who wore a white Makart feather hat, and it was here that the imperial couple received the tributes of the capital of their empire.

Emperor Franz Joseph's "via triumphalis" also saw the procession to mark the monarch's sixtieth jubilee in 1908. This was to be the last great celebration which the many peoples of the Habsburg empire were to hold together.

Any description of this magnificent boulevard would be incomplete if one neglected to mention its alleys and parks, which were an important part of the original plans. The roadway was generously dimensioned for the traffic of the time, and for its entire length was lined by two riding alleys. Nobody has ridden there for a long time now, but the trees still bring green to the heart of the city. As one drives around the Ring, the waving mass of foliage seems to transform the architecture into stage sets. Like historic set pieces, the magnificent buildings appear out of the parkscape. It is a pleasure to walk beneath the shady trees of the alleys, and the parks are an inviting place to rest.

Just beside the Burgtheater is the Volksgarten, which was laid out in 1823 on the site of the rampart destroyed by the departing French in 1809. This park is a delight to visitors, especially in early summer, when it is filled with flowering roses. Towards the Hofburg is the former Corti's Café-Salon built by Peter Nobile. This was where Joseph Lanner and the Strauss brothers once gave concerts. Now the newly renovated pavilion lures visitors in search of refreshment under shady trees after an exhausting sightseeing tour.

Immediately adjacent to the Neue Hofburg is the Burggarten, which until 1918 was reserved for members of the court as the "Kaisergarten". The park has a lot of atmosphere, with its romantic pond and art nouveau glasshouse. Here there is an attractive monument to Wolfgang Amadeus Mozart, one of the most gifted composers ever to have worked in Vienna, but whose genius the Viennese failed to recognise during his lifetime. Incidently, this was a fate which befell many of the great geniuses of this city. The Viennese cabaret artiste Helmut Qualtinger notes that "in Vienna you first have to die before they celebrate you, but then you'll live on long".

The finest park along the Ringstrasse, the Stadtpark, occupies the site of the former glacis. The landscape painter Josef Selleny was involved in the planning of a park created in the genuine English style, with magnificent trees and bushes on expansive lawns and a romantic pond with waterfowl. The art nouveau portal constructed over the River Wien, with steps running down to a riverside promenade and pavilions on either side, looks cheerful and graceful.

Now that we have turned our attention to the subject of "green", let us stay with it a while. Vienna enjoys the reputation of being a garden city. Parks both large and small, alleys lined with magnificent lime trees, acacias and chestnuts, and many tree-covered traffic islands – tiny refuges in the hustle and bustle of the big city – and finally the shady, green courtyards of the old and even more recent houses all go to show that green is an integral part of the city, its grandeur, its spaciousness.

Apart from the parks surrounding the palaces of Schönbrunn and Belvedere, Vienna's most attractive parks include the Augarten, laid out in the French style, the Türkenschanz Park, an English landscape garden on a hilly site with a stalactite cave, waterfalls and an Alpine garden, and the romantic Wertheimstein Park, with its exotic trees, wild shrubs and peaceful ponds. Incidentally, here you will find something unique in the whole of Europe: a "garden for the blind", with guide rails for orientation, signposts in Braille and an acoustic fountain. In Lainz Game Park, a natural park also within city limits, you can walk for many kilometres and observe indigenous wild animals at close quarters.

And, of course, it would not do to forget the famous Vienna Prater, which is mentioned in so many songs. The green splendour of this park-like meadow land is popular with walkers and cyclists looking for relaxation. Vienna's best-known and largest amusement park is also in the Prater.

The Prater was originally an imperial hunting-ground, which in 1766 was thrown open for use by the Viennese populace. Much of the scenic beauty of the park has been preserved to this day. The main alley of the Prater, with its mighty chestnut trees, goes back to plans by Emperor Ferdinand I in the 16th century. At the end of this splendid four and a half kilometre long alley, Isidoro Canevale erected a pleasure-house in 1783. A monster celebration took place in this pavilion during the Congress of Vienna when on 14th October 1814 – the anniversary of the Battle of the Nations near Leipzig – the crowned heads of Europe celebrated the victory over Napoleon with their generals and 18,000 soldiers.

The "Wurstelprater", with its booths, Punch-and-Judy shows and merry-go-rounds, came into being soon after the Prater was opened to the public. Much of the old amusement park has been preserved, despite considerable rebuilding and destruction. It seems a particulary likeable trait of character that the cosmopolitan city of Vienna can become a provincial town where its traditionalistic heart is involved. We find a love of detail, fondly keeping and cherishing the things from great grandfather's time. The astonishing restoration of one of the oldest carousels in Europe is an example. Even "Calafati", a revolving Chinaman erected by Basilio Calafati (1800–1878), has almost become a legend. The figure was destroyed in 1945 and an artificial stone imitation re-erected in 1967.

The Prater was the scene of glamorous festivities until well into the 20th century. There was the annual "Great Spring Festival" with its parade of the carriages of high society, at one and the same time a sort of fashion show. From 1866 onwards, Princess Pauline Metternich, one of the most popular figures of the Viennese aristocracy, held her famous carnival of flowers here. The carnival was attended by members of court, and Viennese onlookers were also able to satisfy their curiosity.

Ever since the townsfolk discovered the countryside as a source of pleasure and recreation, they have been attracted by the verdure around the city. Vienna's charm lies not least in the uniqueness of its situation amidst hills and plains. A gentle range of hills of the Vienna Woods surrounds the city in a wide curve from north-west to south. This landscape, its slopes and valleys partly covered in vineyards and partly in mixed woodland, is still peaceful, still just as idyllic as it was when Franz Schubert composed his delightful dances and Johann Strauss his waltz "Tales from the Vienna Woods". This is an ideal area for contemplative and extensive hikes, and there are any amount of eating-houses, comfortable inns and heuriger wine taverns where tired hikers can refresh themselves. The Viennese have always loved a country outing, with cold schnitzel to eat on the way, or a visit to a heuriger, when you can easily leave the car at home for a change. You first take the tram, and then walk just the right distance to work up a healthy thirst. Lovers of merry company and more contemplative connoisseurs of good wine generally prefer the country taverns, surrounded by vineyards, or the courtyards of whitewashed old wine-growers' houses adorned with flowers. This is far from the crowds of bus tourists every evening, and there are no heuriger singers promoting the sugar-sweet image of "Viennese congeniality" in rather over-sentimental songs. This is where the much-praised Viennese heuriger is still genuine and unadulterated: simple rough or green-painted wooden tables stand beneath shady trees, and they serve natural, dry white wines from the landlord's own vineyards. These wines taste particularly good when you eat a slice of bread and dripping or spicy curd cheese spread with them.

The landscape round about Vienna, with its peaceful villages, ancient monasteries and castles, is certainly one of the loveliest things which Vienna has to offer. You should enjoy the wonderful view of the city and the plain through which the Danube flows the "Höhenstrasse" – this is Vienna at its most attractive. Johann Friedrich Reichardt, the German composer and musical writer whom Goethe so appreciated, committed this impression to paper in 1808: "Nowhere before have I found myself so confirmed and rewarded in my old habit of first becoming acquainted with the surroundings of an attractively situated town as here in Vienna, which lies in the middle of a wonderful and fertile area. I know as yet little about the city and its inhabitants; but fate could force me to leave Vienna this instant, and I would feel well rewarded for the journey by my acquaintanceship with the magnificent countryside around Vienna."

The Danube water-meadows are yet another delightful variant of the lush verdure of the countryside around Vienna. Their grey-green foam accompanies the river on its way across the plain. A natural park will soon maintain and preserve this unique type of landscape in Europe.

But let us return from the beauty of nature, the harmony of the woods and the haunting attraction of the water-meadows to continue our review of the culture and history of Vienna.

At the time of the turn of the century, when the political power of the Habsburg empire was gradually dwindling, there was almost an explosion of creative energy in all spheres of intellectual and cultural life. A golden age had dawned in the cultural history of Vienna which fires the imagination even today.

Vienna was the birthplace of psychoanalysis, a science which brought about a reappraisal of values like no other: it turned the existing moral order upside down – or put it on its feet, as we would say today. However, Sigmund Freud, its creator, was largely rejected in Vienna and recognition came from abroad. To this day, his teachings have not been particularly widely accepted in the very town in which he worked.

The Vienna school of Arnold Schönberg, Alban Berg and Anton Webern represented the most important turning point ever in the history of music: the transition from tonality to atonality and note-row music as a composition technique was not just a new trend, but the beginning of a completely new kind of music.

But in Vienna it is often enough to have invented something, as Hans Weigel once noted. New things are liked here only when they are no longer new, but when they are converging on the classical, when the dissonance of the day before yesterday dissolves into melody and harmony. Thus it is that even today the works of the Schönberg school fail to fill concert halls, and Alban Berg is only very gradually gaining in popularity. This conservative trait in the Viennese character is certainly the result of the predominance of the historical which one feels everywhere in this city.

The architect Adolf Loos, the leading champion of functionalism in Vienna at the turn of the century, was one great innovator. In 1910 he built the house on the corner of Michaelerplatz opposite the Hofburg. Due to its plain façade, the building acquired the nickname of the "house without eyebrows". Emperor Franz Joseph is said to have been so annoyed by it that he never again used the domed entrance to the palace on Michaelerplatz opposite. The revolutionary theories of Loos – his rejection of ornament, and above all his aim of creating a maximum of comfort with a minimum of constructional effort – only bore fruit after the collapse of the monarchy in the council housing of the twenties and thirties, and have retained their validity to this day.

Adolf Loos was rather an outsider who left his mark only on later generations; Josef Maria Olbrich, Josef Hoffmann and Otto Wagner are considered to be the leading exponents of Viennese architecture at the turn of the century. Above all Otto Wagner was a universal architect whose work combined historical, contemporary and futuristic elements. The construction of the Vienna metropolitan railway and the structures that were erected during the regulation of the Danube Canal gave him ample opportunity to develop and try out his new vocabulary. The stations of the metropolitan railway are architectural works of art: they are like temples, elegant and white, ingeniously combining inventiveness and quality workmanship.

Art around 1900 generally reflected the gradual move away from historicism and already displayed many of the trends that would become effective in the 20th century. Geometrical abstraction is only a step away from the painting of Gustav Klimt, with its austere ornamentation of large areas and a tendency to make ornament an end in itself.

In 1897 Vienna's artists joined forces in the "Secession". Their aim was to achieve a new unity of all the arts, and to permeate life in its entirety, all aspects of the daily routine with art. Their interest was focused equally on fashion and furniture, architecture and sculpture, jewellery and tableware, bookbindings and posters. Ornamental and decorative elements were regarded not only as an embellishment, but also as abstracted natural forms and symbols.

Art nouveau proclaimed this unity of all aspects of life, and perhaps it was able to blossom so abundantly in Vienna of all places because the Viennese have always had a propensity for obscuring and effacing the frontiers between art and life.

Within a short space of time, the Secessionists had altered the art scene in Vienna. Their exhibition building, erected by Josef Maria Olbrich in a symbolic and decorative architectural style, soon became a talking point of the Viennese, who irreverently and humorously referred to the dome of the building of gilded laurel sprays as the "golden cabbage".

The most important centre of the Secessionist movement was without doubt the Wiener Werkstätte, which was founded in 1903 by the architect Josef Hoffmann, the painter Kolo Moser and the industrialist Fritz Waerndorfer. This brought together artists and craftsmen working together following a uniform concept. The Wiener Werkstätte had a decisive influence on the development of artistic design in our century.

Josef Hoffmann, the all-round genius of his time, left his mark on the environment of Vienna's middle classes like no other before him, relieving the interior of their homes from the stifling clutter of the Makart age.

For some time now, the products of the Wiener Werkstätte have again been in great demand. They are some of the most sought after and highly valued works from the turn of the century. Apart from the elegant products of the Hoffmann era, with their costly materials and simple geometric shapes, the decorative articles of the twenties are also growing in popularity in a world which has grown tired of purely functional design.

The antique shops of Vienna's inner city offer a wide selection of art nouveau items, and the tendency of the Viennese to describe recent epochs as "good old times" ends with the turn of the century.

A brief look at the literature of this time reveals the Viennese way of life and intellectual attitudes in a manner still applicable today. Hilde Spiel, the author and excellent connoisseur of Viennese literature, has made a fitting analysis of the situation: It was above all Arthur Schnitzler who described the finely spun fabric of Viennese society, and the basic Viennese attitude to life is particularly clearly expressed in his writings – as it was later in the work of Robert Musil and Heimito von Doderer. Scepticism and seemly optimistic resignation, melancholy masked in cheerfulness, escape from reality hidden behind an apparent craving for pleasure, fear of great words and great deeds which is so easily interpreted as insincerity. Musil's "The Man without Characteristics" is fascinated by a multitude of more forceful possibilities compared to a comparatively colourless reality: reality becomes questionable before the power of appearances – a favourite theme of Viennese literature and a fundamental trait of the Viennese character.

In his writings Karl Kraus, the merciless critic and relentless moralist, particularly denounces the non-committance which results from such an attitude, and reveals the insincerity behind the friendly Viennese smile.

The turn of the century was also the heyday of the Viennese coffee-house, which developed into a very special type of cultural institution.

Even in the 18th and 19th century, coffee-houses had been popular meeting places for artists, politicians and journalists. But now the coffee-house became the "nursery" not only of Austrian literature, but also of painting, architecture and music. It was here that new styles and trends were discussed, and the friendships and enmities cultivated which stimulated creativity.

From time to time even men of action mixed among the artists: a certain Lev Bronstein used to sit for hours over a chess board in the famous Café Central. In 1917 he made world history in the Russian revolution as Leon Trotsky.

The number of anecdotes and stories about the Viennese coffee-house and its more or less famous visitors would fill volumes. Many writers, such as Peter Altenberg, Alfred Polgar and Anton Kuh, spent a large part of their lives in such establishments, doing much of their creative work there.

It was they, too, who recognised and defined the nature of the coffee-house as a local place of refuge from an all too harsh reality. Alfred Polgar wrote: "The Café Central is a way of looking at the world, and it is one the very essence of which is not to look at the world."

And Peter Altenberg also admirably characterised this aspect:
"You are worried, about this, or that – go to your coffee-house
She cannot, for some reason, be it ever so plausible, visit you – go to your coffee-house
You have a torn boot – go to your coffee-house
You have a salary of 400 crowns and have spent 500 – go to your coffee-house
You are a civil servant, and would like to have been a doctor – go to your coffee-house
You cannot find the woman for you – go to your coffee-house
You have been contemplating suicide – go to your coffee-house
You hate and despise people, and yet you cannot do without them – go to your coffee-house
Nobody gives you credit any more – go to your coffee-house"

The most famous coffee-houses included the "Central", where Karl Kraus, Peter Altenberg, Egon Friedell and Alfred Polgar were regular customers, and the "Griensteidl", where Hermann Bahr, Arthur

Schnitzler and Hugo von Hofmannsthal came and went. During the period between the wars, Vienna's intellectuals gathered in the "Herrenhof", which was frequented by writers of the calibre of Hermann Broch, Robert Musil, Franz Werfel and Joseph Roth. The Café Museum, meeting-place of painters and architects – Gustav Klimt, Egon Schiele, Oskar Kokoschka, Adolf Loos and Otto Wagner were all regulars there – still exists today. For some years after 1945, Hans Weigel turned the Café Raimund opposite the Volkstheater into a regular meeting-place for the young writers whom he encouraged. The eminent Austrian poetess Ingeborg Bachmann, for example, emerged from this group.

The tradition of a coffee-house for writers and artists is today continued by the "Hawelka" in Dorotheergasse off Graben. This is where Vienna's writers, artists, students and Bohemians meet.

But of course it is not just artists who frequent Vienna's coffee-houses. For some time now, this venerable institution has enjoyed renewed popularity as a place of meditation, a place of leisure and a place of communication. The coffee-house is not a place for people in a hurry: you do not need a bulging wallet if you go there, but you should take your time. A guest can stay there for a morning, an afternoon, or even a whole day over a large or small cup of black or white coffee, a "melange" or an "einspänner". And if he is lucky, the waiter will bring him a fresh glass of water from time to time.

Coffee-house connoisseur and lover Hans Weigel supposes that this cool refreshment has its origins in ancient times. He regards the glass of water as a sign of hospitality, a symbol of the drink of water from the village well with which every traveller was refreshed.

But let us now leave peaceful world of the coffee-house and return once again to the history of the city.

After the First World War Vienna was no longer the centre of a large monarchy, of an empire embracing many peoples, and the painful transition from imperial city to the capital of a small and poor nation had to be made. Over a period of more than half a century – apart from the fateful years 1938–1945 – Vienna became a modern city which had regained its position as a European cultural metropolis. None of the things which are so grandly and naturally set forth in the present townscape – both intellectual and architectural – came easy to the Viennese.

A nostalgic longing for things long past still persists in some areas of social life. To this day, many foods bear the prefix "Kaiser" – "Kaiserschmarrn", "Kaiserfleisch", "Kaisersemmel" – and the expression "Kaiserwetter" is used to describe a particularly glorious day. The Habsburg double-headed eagle and the letters "k. u. k." – standing for imperial and royal – still decorate company name-plates and are still the sign of something particularly exclusive. And thus it is that many peculiarities of the Viennese way of life have their roots in the traditions of the empire, such as the Viennese predilection – often referred to with irony and sarcasm – for all kinds of titles, or their extremely differentiated use of greetings, which allows two individuals meeting one another to establish exactly their social, economic, social and private standing relative to one another. Jörg Mauthe has described this ceremony of greeting and returning greetings in a delightfully humorous way.

The Viennese are always at pains to identify with their past, and to transform history into myth. They do this not merely with an eye to the marketing opportunities for tourism. But in spite of all the glamour and all the burden of the past, since 1945, during the life of the Second Republic, Vienna has found a new conception of itself and a new self-assurance.

Austria has become a comparatively wealthy country. Vienna is today a place in which many political threads run together. The Danube metropolis has become the third official United Nations city after New York and Geneva, and has developed into a congress, conference and trade fair centre of international standing. The United Nations headquarters opened in 1979 on the left bank of the Danube is the seat of numerous international authorities. The complex of glass, steel and concrete symbolises Austria's identity as a neutral country, and her neutrality is politically and morally secured by her role as host to international organisations.

Vienna's art scene is colourful and varied. The numerous galleries, most of them in the inner city, show the liberal attitude of the Viennese to contemporary art from Austria and abroad. The art market flourishes, and private viewings of art exhibitions find an interested public. Vienna particularly cultivates its image as a city of music and theatre, for which the Austrian state is prepared to find money. Though the musical life of the Danube metropolis is splendid, it is marked by conservatism. The world's best known singers, musicians and conductors perform here, and the best orchestras are at home here, but the musical repertoire of Vienna largely extends from Bach and Händel to Mahler and Strauss.

Modern music is not very popular with audiences: Berg, Bartók and Stravinsky are just about tolerated, but do not frequently appear on the programme. The 20th century is getting off to a slow start in the concert halls of Vienna. This inertia is greater in the world of music than anywhere else, and Karl Kraus's remark that "Vienna remains Vienna" takes on a half menacing, half auspicious meaning in this context – auspicious with regard to the high quality of the music performed, menacing with regard to the promotion of new compositions.

Vienna's theatre landscape, on the other hand, is exceptionally varied: the choice ranges from renowned theatres with a long established tradition – such as the State Opera House and the Volksoper, the Burgtheater and the Theater in der Josefstadt, the Volkstheater and the Theater an der Wien – to a multitude of adventurous small theatres that have been set up in cellars, restaurants and cafés. The reason for the dominating role of theatre and music can be found in typically Viennese traits of character – escape from reality and pleasure in appearances, in playing. The same is true of the priority which stars of the music and theatre world enjoy over creative artists.

There are also many alternatives to the established cultural scene: young cabaret artistes and song-makers are exceptionally productive, aggressively giving expression even to the negative sides of life. Danzer, Ambros, Fendrich and Falco, to name but a few, have conquered the hit parades and even succeeded in exporting the Vienna dialect in a way – a new sound, a new export product alongside Strauss waltzes, operetta music and sentimental Viennese songs. Vienna is today a city where youth has an opportunity and a voice, where young talent is promoted in all spheres, by the state, by the City of Vienna, by Austrian Radio, and by the large Austrian banks, the art patrons of our age.

One more word on the nature of the Viennese, whose diverse traits of character have been formed in the course of time by many peoples – Germans and Czechs, Jews and Hungarians, Italians and Slavs. There is hardly a city in Europe where so many national and cultural differences came together as in the capital of the erstwhile Danube monarchy. From this experience of many worlds side by side, from the realisation that there was something to be said for each of them, but that a common denominator could never be found for all of them, there arose a cheerful-pessimistic philosophy of live and let live which, to more severe minds, may also perhaps seem unreliable and superficial. But it has also resulted in an exceptional gift for reconciling differences and combining dissimilarities.

Charm, humour and self-irony are the likeable counterparts to the continuous "raunzen" (a Viennese expression for complaining and finding fault with things), which results from an inner dissatisfaction with reality, from its shortcomings compared to an imagined ideal.

The "golden Viennese heart" and the demonic, ill-natured "Herr Karl" whom the cabaret artiste Helmut Qualtinger has made famous far beyond Vienna indicate the opposing poles in the complicated, contradictory and diverse Viennese character.

But enough talk – Pictures will now give you a much more detailed impression of Vienna and the Viennese. Enjoy yourself on your walk through our city.

Highlights of a visit to Vienna

2·3

25 · 26

39
40

1 From Schönbrunn Palace one looks out over park and hills to the Gloriette. In 1692/93 Johann Bernhard Fischer von Erlach designed a magnificent palace on the instructions of Emperor Leopold I which was to have put Versailles in the shade. The original concept of this great baroque architect is still alive in the entire complex, though in the event – after extensive alteration of the plans by the court architect Nikolaus Pacassi – a more modest building was actually erected under Maria Theresa, who chose Schönbrunn as her summer residence. Thereafter Schönbrunn became the favourite residence of the Habsburgs after the Hofburg. It is linked with the imperial family by many historical events, and much history was made here.
Since the end of the Habsburg rule, the palace has been a much visited museum, and is also used occasionally by the Austrian government for official entertainment.

2·3·6·7 The extensive park of Schönbrunn was originally laid out at the beginning of the 18th century. With the modifications begun in 1765 by Ferdinand Hetzendorf von Hohenberg, the park became one of the finest achievements of French horticulture. Park and palace form a total work of art of astonishingly harmonious unity. The park complements the architecture of the palace: strict geometry predominates in the layout of the areas; lawns and flower beds become artistic ornaments, and any high plants – shrubs, trees and bushes – are transformed into cubic elements by cutting. Between them,

bright white gravelled paths converge on carefully calculated perspective vanishing points, leading to bubbling fountains, with nymphs and Tritons beneath glittering veils of water, or revealing secluded corners in which statues are concealed.

4·5 A view into the rooms of Schönbrunn Palace, where the splendour and opulence reflect the rococo life-style. Empress Maria Theresa engaged artists from all over Europe for the decoration of her living accommodation and rooms of state. At that time the imperial household occupied no fewer than 1,441 rooms and halls. Plate 4 shows the great Rosa Room with inlaid landscape paintings by Josef Rosa (1726–1805) and a painting of Empress Maria Theresa. A salon with a painting of the eighteen year-old Emperor Franz Joseph I (1848) by Anton Einsle can be seen in Plate 5.

8·9·10 The zoological gardens of Schönbrunn, Europe's oldest surviving menagerie, were built to the plans of J. N. Jadot de Ville-Issey at the initiative of Emperor Franz I, Maria Theresa's husband, who took a keen interest in natural science. Only the octogonal central pavilion remains of the old menagerie. Once a breakfast pavilion for the imperial couple, it is now a café and restaurant for visitors.

Severely damaged during the war, the zoo was rebuilt to plans by Michael Engelhart. The zoo is continually being extended and provided with modern outdoor enclosures.

11 Brightly clothed Indian visitors in front of the cascades of the Neptune fountain. The fountain at the foot of the Gloriette hill is richly adorned with figures and is the work of the sculptors Franz Anton Zaunder and Wilhelm Bleyer. The dramatic group surmounting the fountain represents a scene from mythology: Thetis begs Neptune to help her son Achilles on his journey to Troy. The background to the gushing fountains during the summer months is formed by naiads and Tritons subduing horses.

12 Wide expanses of lawn with magnificent flower beds spread out before the garden front of Schönbrunn Palace. The differentiated baroque facade is given an individual note by the delicate sweep of the outdoor staircase and the balcony on pillars in front of the state rooms of the palace.

13·14 Schönbrunn yellow and winter white – a fascinating colour composition in the cour d'honneur of Schönbrunn Palace. The two fountains which adorn the large square courtyard were created by Johann Baptist Hagenauer and Franz Anton Zauner in the year 1776. Hagenauer's sculptures symbolise the union of the kingdoms of Galicia and Lodomeria with the grand principality of Transylvania, while Zauner's allegorical stone figures represent the Danube, Inn and Enns Rivers.

15 The Gloriette appears to be sinking into the snow. The crowning glory of Schönbrunn was erected by Ferdinand Hetzendorf von Hohenberg in 1775. Built in early classical style with airy, elegant arcades, the Gloriette dominates the park. From here you can enjoy a wonderful view of the park and palace, the city and the Vienna Woods.

16 Belvedere palace: a jewel of Austrian baroque architecture. Prince Eugene of Savoy, the great conqueror of the Turks, had this palace built as a summer residence and for his old age by the same architect who had served him as a fortifications engineer on his campaigns: Johann Lukas von Hildebrandt. Standing on a hill to the south of the city, the palace was originally in open countryside when it was built. Between the two palaces, the Upper and the Lower Belvedere, is a magnificent park. The Lower Belvedere, a long, gracious, single-storey building with a cour d'honneur, was the palace in which the prince resided. Across the park which rises gently from the Lower Belvedere, one has a view of the Upper Belvedere. This palace, which was used for entertainment only, was erected to Hildebrandt's plans in the years 1721–1724. The incomparable elegance of the long building, extending between four delicate domed corner pavilions, bears witness to the boundless imagination of this master of the high baroque style.

The south front is reflected in the lake constructed in front of it: the palace becomes a fairy-tale castle supported by its own shimmering reflection. Today the Belvedere houses the "Austrian Gallery", where art lovers can find a cross-section of Austrian painting and sculpture from the Middle Ages to the present day.

17–20 Winter spreads its icy tentacles over coats of arms, roof sculptures and sphinx: details of the Upper Belvedere.

21 Lions symbolising royal magnanimity and dignity support the coat of arms of Savoy, which is topped by a prince's crown.

22 The garden front of the Upper Belvedere. Prince Eugene was a highly educated, art-loving and wealthy client, so architects and artists from all fields were able to plan liberally and realise dreams. The Frenchman Claude de Fort du Plessy was commissioned with the interior design, but everywhere one can feel the guiding hand of Hildebrandt, who had an army of Viennese artists, craftsmen and decorators at his disposal.

23·25·26·27 The magnificent gardens which extend in terraces between the two palaces were designed by the famous landscape gardner Dominique Girard. Executed entirely in the French style, with trimmed hedges and flower beds, with sculptured fountains and open staircases, the park is a veritable festival hall beneath the open sky.

24 The famous panoramic view from the Upper Belvedere across the park and fountains towards Vienna and the hills to the north of the city.

28 The gaze of the sphinx – smiling inscrutably over the course of time – directs us over the roofs of the city.

29 A view of the great marble hall in the Lower Belvedere, where the original figures from Raphael Donner's Providence Fountain on Neuer Markt can be seen.

Austrian baroque works of art are displayed in the rooms of the Lower Belvedere, many of which are elaborately and sumptuously decorated.

30 The gallery in the Upper Belvedere houses the collection of Austrian art from the end of the baroque era to the present day. Prominent painters from the Biedermeier, historicist and art nouveau periods are represented here.

31–35 The Spanish Riding School: classical horsemanship at its best. The white stallions, full of grace, strength and elegance, are not just a "Viennese cliché", they are an exquisite elite which has carried the fame of the Spanish Riding School around the world. Nobody should miss the great experience of a performance. The Spanish Court Riding School – the oldest riding school in the world – goes back to Emperor Maximilian II's "Spanish Riding Stable", in which only horses of Spanish descent were accommodated. The Lippizaners are descended from these horses. The court stud farm at Lippiza near Trieste was founded in 1580. After the First World War, the horses were transferred to the stud farm at Piber near Graz in Styria, where – with several interruptions during the Second World War – they have since been bred.

The Lippizaner stallions are given intensive training and taught haute école, which they apparently master with perfect ease, enabling them to perform the most intricate steps with impudence.

The performances of the Lippizaners take place in the winter riding school of the Hofburg, which was built for Emperor Karl VI by Joseph Emanuel Fischer von Erlach in 1728–1735. In the course of more than two hundred years of history, the magnificent fifty-five metre long riding hall has been the scene of glamorous festivities, at the time of Maria Theresa and during the Congress of Vienna. Today it is used almost exclusively to display the skills of the Lippizaners. When these fine horses and their riders prance gracefully through the baroque hall, effortlessly rise on their hind legs for the "levade", and spring spiritedly through the air during the "capriole", it may be possible to guess how much work has gone into their agility.

The horses are stabled in the Stallburg, a Renaissance palace which is part of the Hofburg. Each horse has its own box with a marble manger. A plaque with a brass frame gives each stallion's name and year of birth, and in the corridor leading to the stables the names and dates of famous Lippizaners are engraved in marble.

36–40 The Vienna Boys' Choir is more than just a choir. It is an institution which can look back on a long tradition in the musical life of the city. The boys' choir was founded in 1498 by the art-loving Emperor Maximilian I, who thus completed his staff of music makers following the Dutch pattern. The boys sang at high masses, processions, coronations, the imperial diet, and at the emperor's table. The choir was disbanded following the collapse of the monarchy. Court chaplain Josef Schnitt founded the choir anew in 1924 with great personal effort. A financial basis for the choir was also established by public performances and extended concert tours. Instead of the old court uniform of cadets or pages, from this time on the boys wore the sailors' suits which were the usual Sunday dress of the children of the higher classes. Since 1948 the boys' choir has been housed in the Augarten Palace, a baroque building dating from the 17th century. Music has always played a central role at the palace: the young Mozart gave concerts here, the seventeen year-old piano virtuoso Beethoven played here, and Franz Liszt, Richard Wagner and Johann Strauss were also regular visitors.

One custom has been preserved from the days of the empire: to this day the boys still sing Sunday mass in the chapel of the Hofburg as they did at the time of Emperor Maximilian.

A magnificent tribute . . .

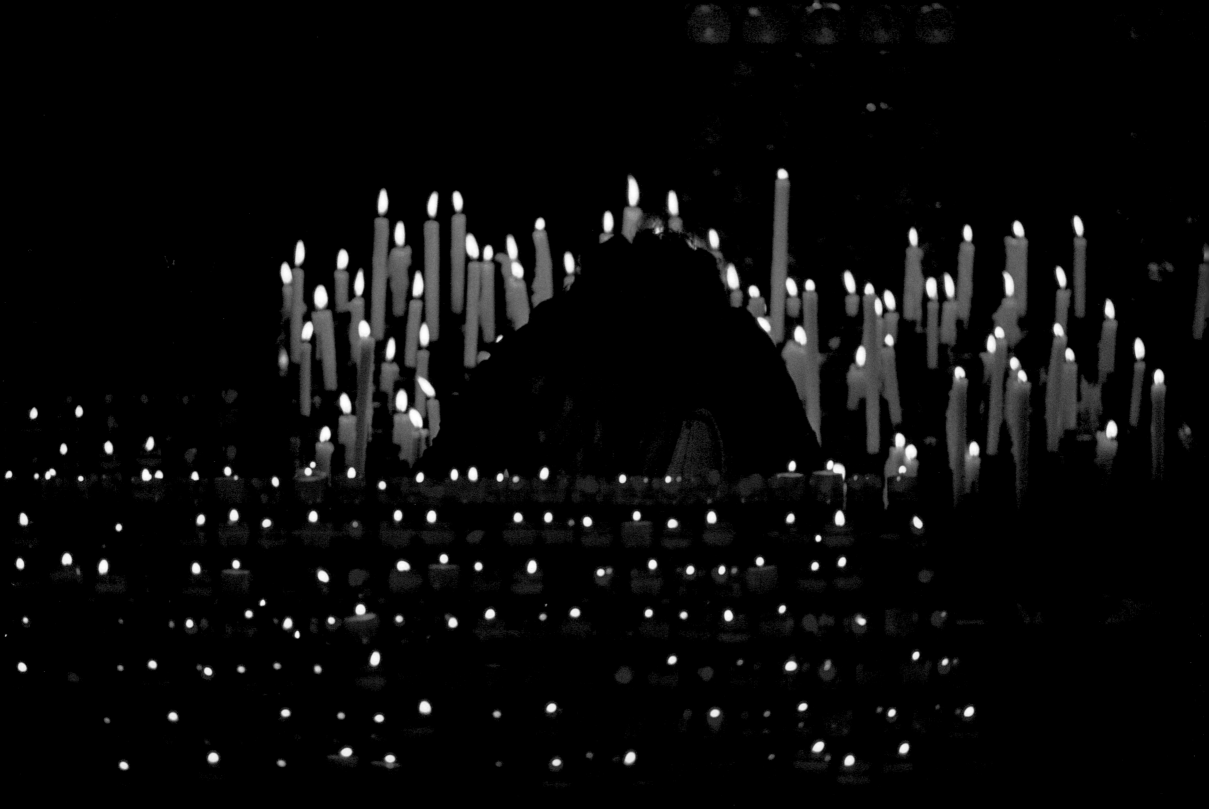

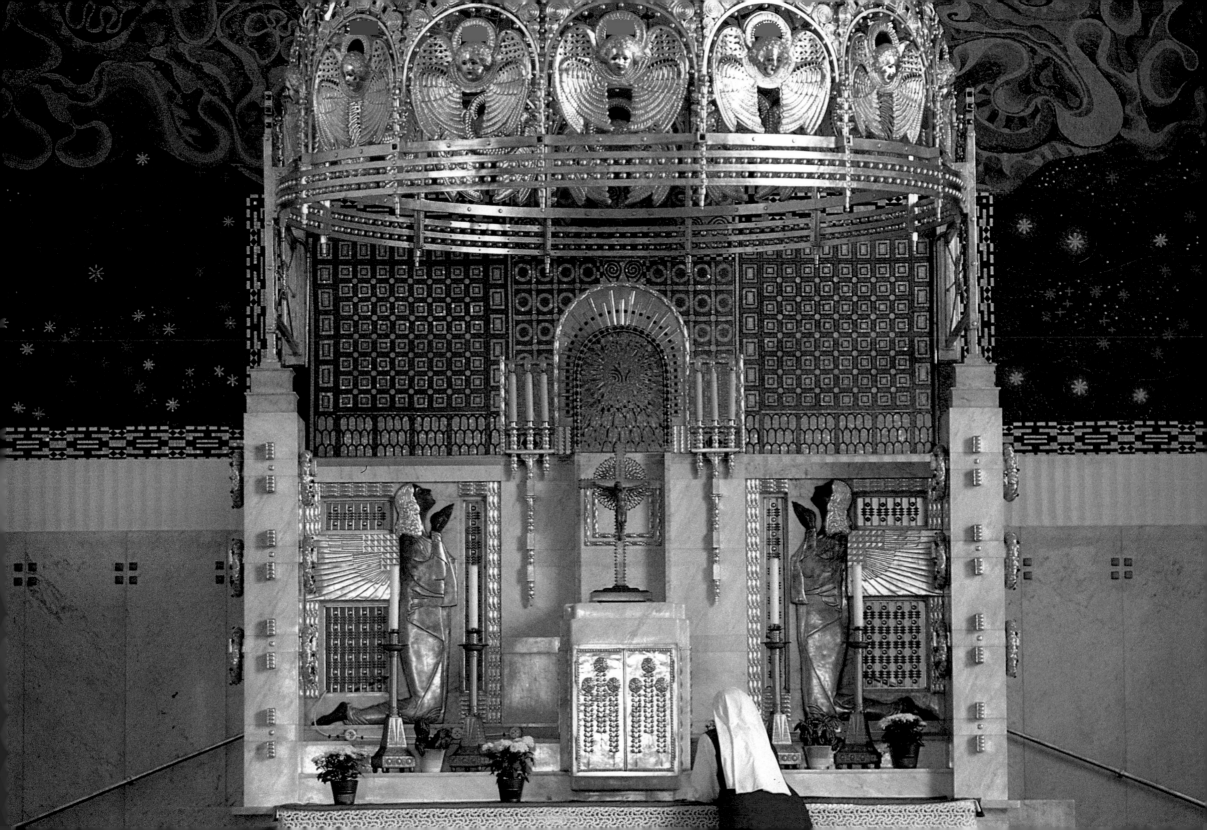

41 Some of the finest landmarks of Vienna are its churches, which stand out against the skyline of the city. However, they are all outshone by St. Stephan's Cathedral with its soaring south tower, affectionately known as "Steffel" by the Viennese.

Vienna's archiepiscopal cathedral was originally founded in 1147 as the Parish Church of St. Stephan outside the walls of the city – which were partly still the old Roman ones. Of the first Roman building, only the western section with the two "Heiden" towers and the great portal is still standing today, and the cathedral in its present state goes back to the Gothic rebuilding commenced in 1304. The task of incorporating the Roman west façade was cleverly solved by the construction of the two chapels with the "Heiden" towers on either side of the great portal.

The mighty south tower with a height of 136.7 metres was begun in 1359 and completed in 1433 by Hans von Prachatitz. The tower was added beside the transept and rises straight out of the ground, soaring majestically over the roofs towards the sky. This loftiness is underlined by hundreds of finials, steep gables, pinnacles and delicate tracery. The builder of the tower mastered the problems of structural engineering with astonishing daring, appearing to have overcome the laws of gravity. For over half a millennium now "Steffel" has towered above the city, and Viennese songs refer to it as a benevolent old gentleman looking down unperturbed on the hustle and bustle around him.

The north tower – also known as Eagle's Tower – was originally planned as a counterpart to the south tower. It was begun in 1450 by Hans Puchspaum, but construction work was stopped in 1511, and half a century later the tower received its octagonal cupola.

The plan to complete the north tower was revived again in the 17th century, but fortunately did not come to fruition, for what would Vienna have been like with two Steffel's?

The Eagle's Tower now houses the "Pummerin", Vienna's largest bell, with a weight of around 20 tonnes. The bell was originally cast from captured Turkish cannons, but shattered into pieces during the fire at the end of the Second World War. The new bell was cast from the fragments, and now its solemn, deep peal sounds again.

42 The mighty Gothic pitched roof, together with the dominating south tower give St. Stephan's Cathedral an unmistakable appearance. The pattern of colourfully glazed tiles can be seen on views of the city from the Middle Ages. The imperial double-headed eagle and the year 1831 were added in the 19th century when the chancel was roofed over. The roof was destroyed in 1945, but subsequently reconstructed again exactly like the original. The magnificent wooden timbering of the roof, a masterpiece of Gothic carpentry, was replaced by a steel structure which retained the characteristic shape of the roof.

43 The square round about St. Stephan's was once a cemetery, the "Stephansfreithof", which was abandoned by Emperor Karl VI following a fire in 1732. Numerous gravestones were set in the walls of the cathedral. In the year 1781 the Mary Magdelene Chapel in the cemetery burned down and was not rebuilt. The foundations of the chapel were unearthed in excavations carried out by the department for the preservation of historical monuments during the construction of the underground railway in 1972/7. After completion of the underground railway station on Stephansplatz, the ground plan of this cemetery chapel was marked out in the paving. During the excavations they also discovered the Gothic Virgil Chapel of 1304, which is now a small museum accessible from Stephansplatz underground railway station.

44 Sunk in prayer before the sacrificial candles of the Maria Pötsch altar of St. Stephan's Cathedral. The iconic miracle painting from Maria Pötsch in Upper Hungary was brought to Vienna in 1697 by order of the emperor and is still venerated to this day.
St. Stephan's Cathedral is the finest achievement of Austrian high and late Gothic architecture, the most mature work of local craftsmen. On entering through the great portal, the visitor finds himself in a spacious nave with soaring clustered columns, immersed in a mysterious twilight. The interior of the cathedral contains a rich treasure of paintings, altars and monuments. Particularly worthy of mention are the exceptionally beautiful Gothic "Servants' Madonna" (about 1340), the Wiener Neustadt altar, a richly carved winged altar from the middle of the 15th century, and the tomb of Emperor Friedrich III, created by Niclas Gerhaert van Leyden in red marble and one of the finest tombs of the Gothic era.

45 The pulpit by the second column of the nave on the left is the veritable "jewel of St. Stephan's", a delightful piece of late Gothic workmanship by Anton Pilgram (1510–1515). The stone takes on a lacy quality, and the heaviness of the material seems disappear – the late Gothic stonemason's art at the peak of perfection. At the foot of the pulpit a self-portrait of Anton Pilgram – slightly hidden beneath the stairs – peers out at us as if from a window. This carving chiselled in stone is certainly one of the most famous portraits from the Middle Ages (1512).

46–49 The traditional palm blessing and palm procession in the inner city of Vienna. On Palm Sunday, the Sunday before Easter, the Archbishop of Vienna, accompanied by the chapter of the cathedral and the clergy of the diocese of St. Stephan, celebrates the liturgy with the faithful. The palm branches are blessed by the Trinity Column on Graben, and from there the procession wends its way to the cathedral.

50 Graben was originally a defensive ditch until well into the 12th century. After it was filled in, it served as a busy food market for several centuries. Depending on the goods sold there, the name varied from "Fleischgraben" to "Kräutermarkt" and even "Grüner Markt". During the baroque era, Graben became the centre of life in the big city. Palais Bartolotti-Partenfeld, the work of Lukas von Hildebrandt, dates from this time. Most of the other buildings were erected in the second half of the 19th century.
Today Graben is Vienna's most exclusive shopping street after Kärntner Strasse, and in 1971 the first pedestrian precinct was established there, initially for a trial period.

51 The statue of Saint Rupert beside the Church of St. Rupert. The Church of St. Rupert, an almost modest little church compared to Vienna's many baroque church buildings, is the oldest place of worship in Vienna. It was probably founded by a townsman as early as the 9th, but no later than the 11th century on the site of an old Roman watch-tower. The foundations consist of Roman stonework, while the nave and the lower part of the tower were built in the 11th century. The tower was subsequently heightened in the 12th century. Thereafter pious aristocratic and middle class individuals saw to the maintenance of the church, which has never attracted the attention of the general public. The original Roman forms were restored in the course of extensive renovation work carried out in the years 1934—1936.

52 The focal point of Graben is the Trinity or Plague Column erected by Emperor Leopold I during the plague in 1679 as the result of a vow. The column was originally only of wood. It was here that Father Abraham a Sancta Clara gave his famous sermon of repentance "Merk's Wien" in the year 1680. The present column of stone was made to designs by Matthias Rauchmiller and consecrated in 1693. Johann Bernhard Fischer von Erlach also worked on the base. The ethereal obelisk of clouds and the gilded sculptured tip of the Trinity Column are the work of Paul Strudel, to a design by Ludovico Burnacini.

53 The history of St. Peter's Church makes it one of the most interesting churches in Vienna. According to the latest research, it is of Roman origin. The first place of worship on this site was a hall church dating from the 4th century which was rebuilt in the 11th century. On the other hand, the relief of Rudolf Weyr on the south front reminds us of the legend according to which the church was founded by Charlemagne the Great in the year 792. The old church had a mighty tower which is shown in Jakob Hufnagel's engraving of 1609. Emperor Leopold I ordered the church to be demolished when it fell into disrepair. In 1702 he laid the foundation stone of the baroque building which was begun by Gabriele Montani and probably completed by Lukas von Hildebrandt. The very unusual concave façade with the crowning dome between diagonally positioned corner towers looks extremely charming. Like St. Stephan's, the old church was surrounded by a cemetery, the "Petersfreithof", one of the oldest cemeteries in Vienna, which was abandoned under Emperor Joseph II. The church is rich in art treasures: a dome fresco "Assumption of the Virgin Mary" by Michael Rottmayr, paintings and figural decoration by Johann Georg Schmidt, Antonio Galli-Bibiena, Martino Altomonte, Anton Schoonjans and others.

54 The Votive Church was the first building along the Ringstrasse. The church was erected by Heinrich von Ferstel in 1856—1879 on the outside edge of the glacis, a strip of open land in front of the city walls which was left undeveloped for military reasons. Ferstel's work is entirely in the style of a French Gothic cathedral. The church, whose delicate silhouette with the two slender towers can be seen on any panoramic view of the city, is one of the most delightful neo-Gothic church buildings of the 19th century. The church was built in gratitude to Providence for an unsuccessful attempt on the life of Emperor Franz Joseph I on 18th February 1853.

55 The original, very noteworthy glass windows of the church, to designs by Eduard Steinle and Josef Führich, were largely destroyed in 1945 and have now been replaced by copies. The church was initially conceived as a last resting place for famous Austrians, but this plan did not progress any further than the altar tomb for count Niklas Salm, one of the defendants of Vienna during the first Turkish siege in 1529. The attractive sarcophagus (1533) was moved here from the Church of St. Dorothy and can now be found in the baptistery.

56 Art nouveau and high baroque on Karlsplatz: the former metropolitan railway station building, and in the background the Church of St. Charles Borromeo.
Otto Wagner built Vienna's metropolitan railway system in the years 1894–1901, and many of his station buildings still exist today. In the course of the complete rearrangement of Karlsplatz during the construction of the underground railway, the two station buildings were dismantled and re-erected after appropriate restoration by the architect Jan Koci. They now no longer serve their original purpose: one of the pavilions houses a café, the other a documentation of Otto Wagner's metropolitan railway installations – both open only during the summer.

These pavilions are a good example of Otto Wagner's principle of allowing the beauty of the material to speak for itself.

57·58 The Church of St. Charles Borromeo originally stood on the other side of the Wien River – elevated above the city – in the middle of grassland. Although the church is today flanked by buildings to the left and right of it, its front is unobstructed in front of the artificial pond which was laid out during the rearrangement of Ressel Park and embellished with a sculpture by Henry Moore.
Ressel Park, with its trees and monuments, gives the mighty church the space which a baroque building needs to be seen to good effect.
The church, which is dedicated to Charles Borromeo, the saint of the plague, is Johann Bernhard Fischer von Erlach's supreme achievement, and can be regarded as one of the most significant examples of baroque architecture anywhere. It was intended to symbolise the universal title of the church and the Austrian empire in the imperial capital. In front of the enormous oval dome is a Greek temple, on either side of which is a Roman triumphal column with spiral reliefs winding up it. The similiarity to the Trajan columns in Rome is unmistakable. The idea of placing two such mighty columns beside an equally mighty church is certainly what makes this work a unique creation of this era.

59·60 The monumental Church of St. Leopold at Steinhof is one of the most outstanding buildings in the Vienna art nouveau style and is considered to be the most personal work of Otto

Wagner (1904—1907). From the outside, the motif of nails in marble blocks is reminiscent of the Post Office Savings Bank building, which was built at the same time. The dome of gilded copper sheeting is very unusual and can be seen from far and wide. The large semicircular window with the glass mosaic above the main portal is the work of Kolo Moser, as is the glass painting of the windows.
The magnificent interior design of the church is entirely uniform in art nouveau style; the altar mosaics were created by Rudolf Jettmar.

61 The light plays fascinatingly on the two figures beneath the dome of the Michael wing of the Hofburg in the passageway leading to the inner courtyard.

62 Atlantes, which take their name from Atlas, the supporter of the heavens, were popular architectural motifs in the baroque era. Used on the portals of palaces, beneath balconies, in stairways and winter gardens, these subjugated giants, slaves and sylvans are allegorical allusions to the power of the princely builder.

63·65 The delightful Johann Strauss monument by Edmund Hellmer (1921) in the Stadtpark. The King of the Waltz is conducting, violin in hand, surrounded by the genii of his art. Fred Hennings had the following to say about this world famous master of Viennese music: ". . . His compositions are imbued with the Olympian ethereality which one otherwise finds only in Mozart . . . the leading violinists in the first movement of the Ringstrasse Symphony were Emperor Franz Joseph and the Waltz King Johann Strauss the Younger."

64 White marble shines against a green backdrop: the Schubert memorial in the Stadtpark – a tribute to the great composer, to the quintessence of Viennese music, with its combination of light-hearted gaiety and melancholy, sweetness and sorrow. The monument donated by the Vienna Men's Choral Society was erected in 1872 by Carl Kundmann with the assistance of Moritz von Schwind. The base is the work of Theophil Hansen.

66·67 The Russian Orthodox Church was built to plans by the Petersburg architect Grigori Kotoff by Luigi von Giacomelli (1893—1899). The two-storey brick building in the Russian late Byzantine style has five domes with lanterns and bulbous cupolas. The interior is well worth seeing, executed in oriental cypress wood.

68 A great master in the evening light: the Goethe monument on Opernring. The prince of poets is enthroned on a magnificent chair on a base with three steps. This dignified monument was donated by the Vienna Goethe Association and created by Edmund Hellmer in 1900.

Along the Ringstrasse

77 · 78

81·8

99 · 100

DER·ZEIT·IHRE·KVNST·
DER·KVNST·IHRE·FREIHEIT

VER·SACRVM·

69 A view from St. Stephan's Cathedral: in the foreground the Michael wing of the Hofburg, the tower of St. Michael's Church and the parliament buildings.

70 A sea of lilac in front of the widely curved wing of the Neue Burg on Heldenplatz.
The Vienna Hofburg, the former imperial residence, is an enormous complex of individual buildings erected over the course of 700 years. By and large the three main courtyards – Schweizerhof, "In der Burg" and Heldenplatz – represent three different stages of development: Gothic, baroque and historicism. The Neue Burg was erected in Renaissance style between 1881 and 1913 under the supervision of Gottfried Semper, Karl Hasenauer, Emil Förster, Friedrich Ohmann and Ludwig Baumann. Today this very extensive building contains several important museums, such as the Ethnological Museum and many of the collections belonging to the Museum of Fine Arts – the Weapons Collection and the Collection of Ancient Musical Instruments – and the Ephesus Museum containing the finds from the first excavations made by the Austrian Archaeological Institute. The reading room and catalogue room of the Austrian National Library are also in the same building.

71·72 Austrian National Day on Heldenplatz. This is one of Vienna's most beautiful squares, set against the magnificent backdrop of the Leopold wing of the old Hofburg, which contained the living accommodation of Empress Maria Theresa, and the extended

façade of the Neue Burg. The two prominently positioned equestrian statues of the "heroes" Prince Eugene and Archduke Carl give the square its name, and were created by Anton Dominik Fernkorn. The monument to Archduke Carl, the victor over Napoleon in the Battle of Aspern in 1809, is a particularly bold composition.
The magnificent view of the Ringstrasse from Heldenplatz is positively delightful: a row of the most splendid buildings imaginable stands out in spectacular perspective against the skyline, from the outer gate of the Hofburg to the parliament buildings and the town hall, and on to the Burgtheater. In clear weather one can also see the blue chain of hills of the Vienna Woods.

73 The monument to Emperor Franz Joseph I, one of many reminders of the House of Habsburg in Vienna, was only erected in the Burggarten in 1957. Although the nationalists in various parts of the empire may have regarded him as an oppressor, in the minds of the Viennese, the emperor with the bushy side-whiskers in uniform with a field mashall's baton is something of a father figure, a "kind, good old gentleman" – as it says in a song by Ralph Benatzky. The political unrest and nationalistic turbulence of a discordant multi-nation empire could not be mastered with his conservative attitude. Nevertheless, the country experienced a long period of peace during his 68-year rule, and Vienna became one of the most splendid capitals in Europe.
His hard personal fate – he lost a son by suicide, a brother by execution, a wife and successor by assassins' daggers and revolvers – aroused and still arouses sympathy.

74 The Austrian imperial crown – a work of art of exquisite beauty and symbol of the Habsburgs' power and might – can be admired in the Treasury.

This crown of Emperor Rudolf II (1552–1612) was created in 1602 in the imperial workshop in Prague. It is 28.6 cm in height, and is made of gold, enamel, pearls, rubies and a saphire above the cross at the top. Three reliefs on facets of the crown depict the coronations of Rudolf II: as Emperor of the Holy Roman Empire, as King of Hungary and as King of Bohemia. The fourth relief glorifies Rudolf as the vanquisher of the Turks. The successors of Emperor Rudolf II kept the crown in the treasury of the House of Habsburg, and it was only worn occasionally by rulers. In 1804, after the establishment of the Austrian imperial family, it became the crown of state of the hereditary Habsburg monarchy and the Crown of Austria.

75 The Prince Eugene monument on Heldenplatz: the great conqueror of Turks has sat on horseback here since 1865. The bronze statue comes from the workshop of the sculptor and ore founder Anton Dominik Fernkorn, while the ornamentation of the marble base was designed by the architect Eduard van der Nüll, one of the builders of the opera house.

76 The magnificent court library on the present-day Josefsplatz was erected for Emperor Karl VI by Joseph Emanuel Fischer von Erlach to plans by his father, the great Johann Bernhard Fischer von Erlach.

This enormous baroque building is still a part of the Hofburg complex. The two side wings were built in the second half of the 18th century by Nikolaus Pacassi. Beneath the dome of the main building is the majestic Gala Hall, which is one of the most beautiful library halls in the world. The enormous inventory of the library runs to millions of volumes, and also includes the libraries of famous collectors, such as the library of Prince Eugene and volumes from the monasteries dissolved by Joseph II. It is also worth mentioning the famous papyrus collection and the collection of manuscripts.

77 The Theseus Temple, a piece of Greece in the Volksgarten, is a popular meeting-place for young people in summer.

Peter Nobile erected this imitation of the Theseion in Athens in 1820–1823. Anton Canova's mighty marble sculpture of Theseus doing battle with a centaur purchased by Emperor Franz II (I) in Rome originally stood here: the statue was moved to the Museum of Fine Arts in 1890. Today the building is used occasionally for exhibitions.

78 "The Victor", a bronze statue of a young athlete before the Theseus Temple created by Josef Müllner in 1921.

79 The Christmas Market on Rathausplatz, with its surging crush of booths and shoppers, is an inviting place to go on a Christmas shopping spree. Here you can buy unusual Christmas tree decorations, candles, pastries and toys of all kinds.

80 The Burgtheater: still one of the leading German language theatres. The last of the Ringstrasse buildings to go up, the new Burgtheater was built opposite the town hall – on the site of the old Löwel bastion – by the architects Gottfried Semper and Karl Hasenauer in the late Italian Renaissance style. It was the successor of the old Hofburg Theater on Michaelerplatz, which was founded by Maria Theresa and made a national theatre by Joseph II. The old Hofburg Theatre closed its doors on 13th October 1888, and on 14th October 1888 the new theatre opened with Grillparzer's "Esther" and Schiller's "Wallensteins Lager". Above the windows of the central building are huge busts of Calderón, Shakespeare, Molière, Schiller, Goethe, Lessing, Halm, Grillparzer and Hebbel. Many eminent names are associated with the management of this and the old theatre: Josef Schreyvogel, Heinrich Laube, Adolf Wildbrand, Anton Wildgans. There are also many actors of international standing: Charlotte Wolter, Alexander Moissi, Josef Kainz, Werner Krauss, Raoul Aslan. The present company of actors includes several from the great Max Reinhardt school. Heinrich Laube once remarked: Stay in Vienna for a year and you will see at the Burgtheater everything classical or contemporary which German literature has brought forth for the theatre for a century. This remark is still true today.

81 The concerts in the arcaded courtyard of Vienna's town hall focus chiefly on the traditional classical and romantic musical repertoire, and are one of the popular cultural events in Vienna during the summer.

82·83 Friedrich von Schmidt modelled his magnificent new town hall on famous medieval civic buildings such as the town hall in Brussels. The imposing neo-Gothic building has a central projection with a high tower, at the top of which stands the "Rathausmann", a 3.4 metre high armoured copper standard-bearer. Apart from the municipal authorities, the town hall also houses the municipal archives and the municipal library. Of the many halls and rooms, it is particularly worth mentioning the People's Hall on the ground floor and the great Festival Hall on the first floor, with ten monumental statues of historic personalities and an apsidal niche at either end for an orchestra. This is where the Press Club's Concordia Ball – one of the highlights of the Vienna ball calendar – is held in June each year.

84 The Rathaus Park, laid out in 1872/73 by the town gardener Rudolf Sieböck, lies on either side of the access road between the Burgtheater and the town hall. Thanks to its many exotic trees, the park is considered to be one of Vienna's most attractive. It is adorned with countless monuments and two fountains.

85 A quadriga on the parliament buildings stands out against a clear spring sky. The parliament buildings, originally the seat of both chambers of the imperial parliament, were erected by Theophil von Hansen, professor at the Academy of Fine Arts, in 1873 after a competition. In this building, the Dane Theophil Hansen, indeed the

houses with façades of a novel beauty which were a great sensation among his contemporaries. Sprigs of flowers and leaf ornaments, the typical decorative forms of art nouveau, cover the famous "Majolikahaus" at no. 40 Linke Wienzeile. The entire building is clad in weather resistant tiles.

The adjoining house at no. 38 is no less magnificent. The graphic artist and painter Kolo Moser designed the stucco decorations on the façade: golden medallions and palm branches. In 1973 the stuccowork of the façade was renovated true to the original by the federal department for the preservation of historical buildings. The "Exclaiming Woman", a roof-top figure by Othmar Schimkowitz, seems to proclaim the new art nouveau joie de vivre: the unity of art and life, a life in beauty.

99·100 The Secession – a landmark of Viennese art nouveau and one of the most charming museums in the Danube metropolis – appears in its original glory after extensive renovation by the architect Adolf Krischantiz.

Josef Olbrich designed this strictly cubic building with its individual crowning dome of gilded laurel branches. It was built in 1897/98 as an exhibition pavilion and a symbol of the new art for the "Secession", an association of Viennese artists.

101·102 One of the most striking works of Otto Wagner is the Post Office Savings Bank building on Georg Coch Platz (1904–1906). In this late work the great master was already striving for purely functional design. The rhythmically arranged nailing in the marble and granite slabs of the façade is the only decoration. The architect's artistic maturity is revealed in this work in the harmonic conformity of shape and material. The main hall of the Post Office Savings Bank is famous, drawing its indirect light from a magnificent glass structure. High on the roof stands the severe art nouveau angel created in aluminium by the sculptor Othmar Schimkowitz as an emphatic mark of the art nouveau view of the solemnity and sanctity of art.

103 The building of the Vienna Urania was erected in 1909 to plans by the architect Max Fabiani, a pupil of Otto Wagner. The Urania takes its name – that of the Greek Muse of astronomy – from the adjacent observatory. This adult education centre, with its many courses, lectures and events of all kinds, is an important place for the cultivation of intellectual and artistic culture for all sections of the Viennese population.

A pulsing metropolis

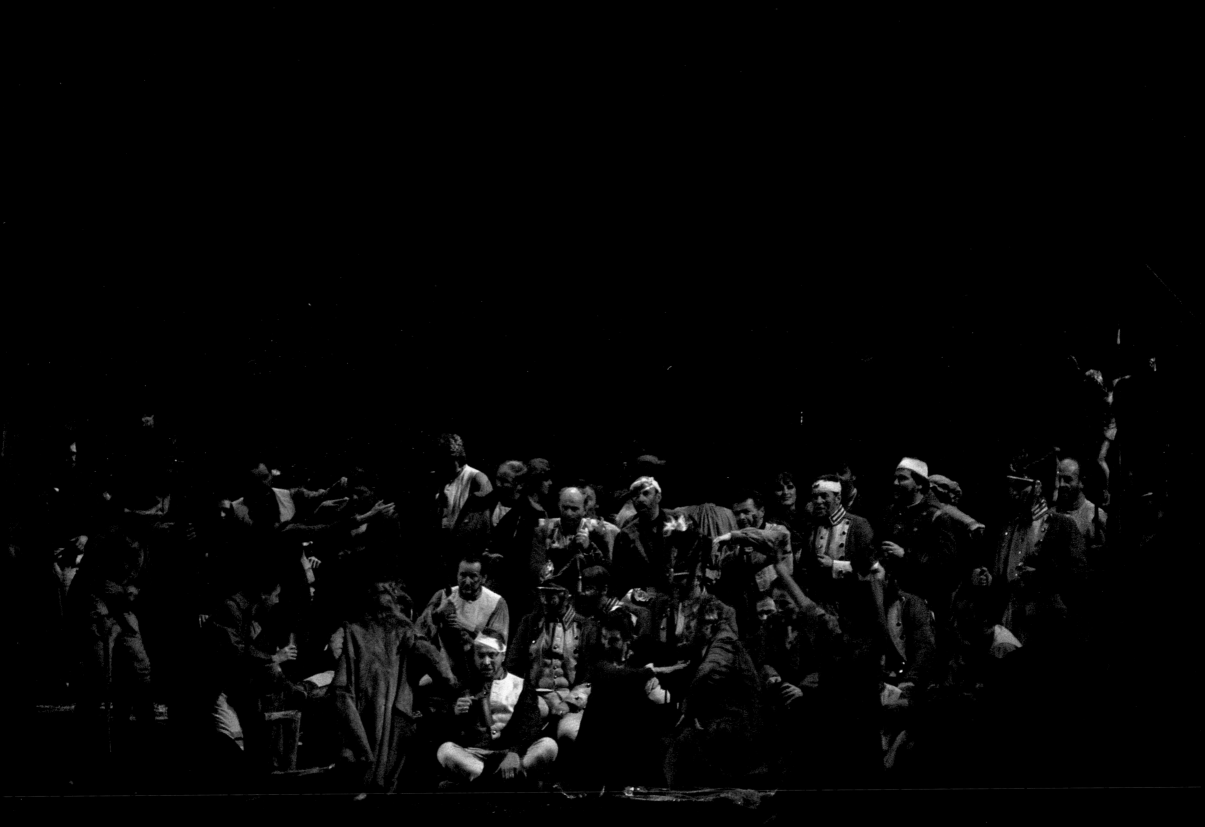

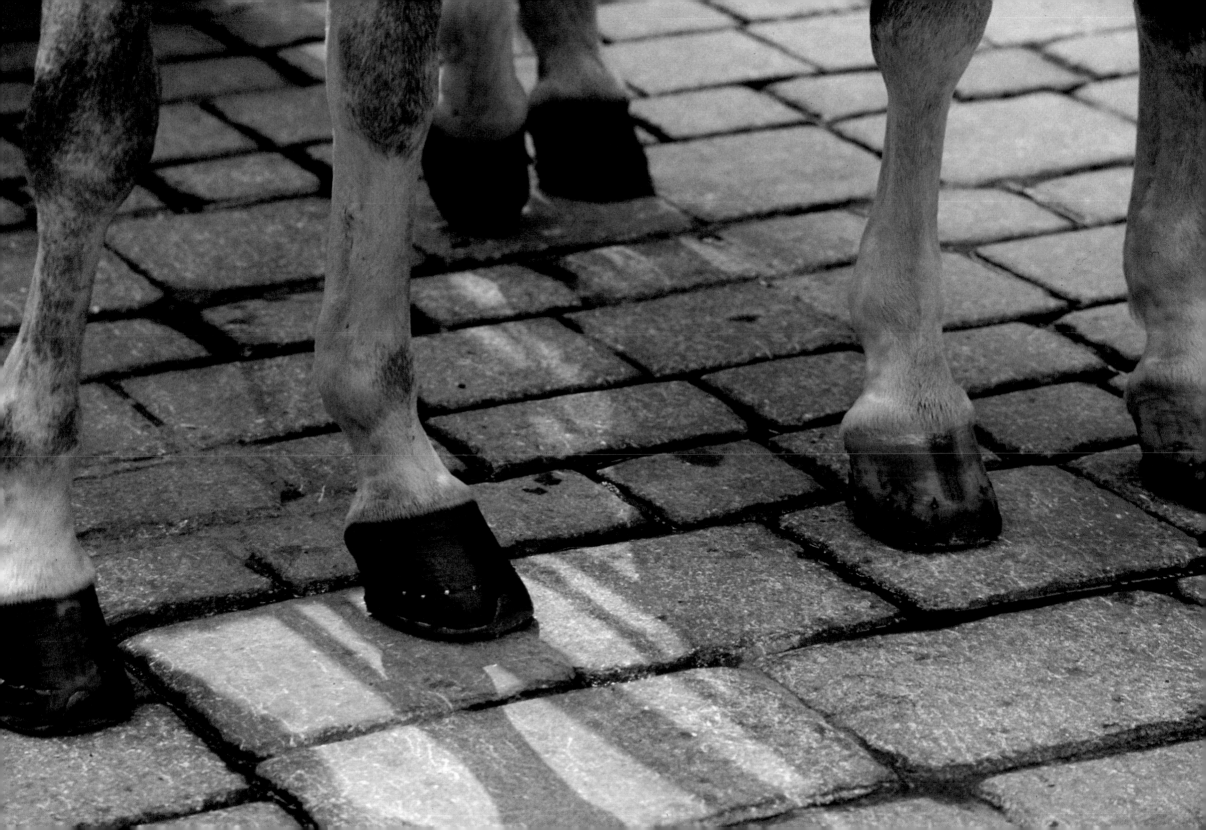

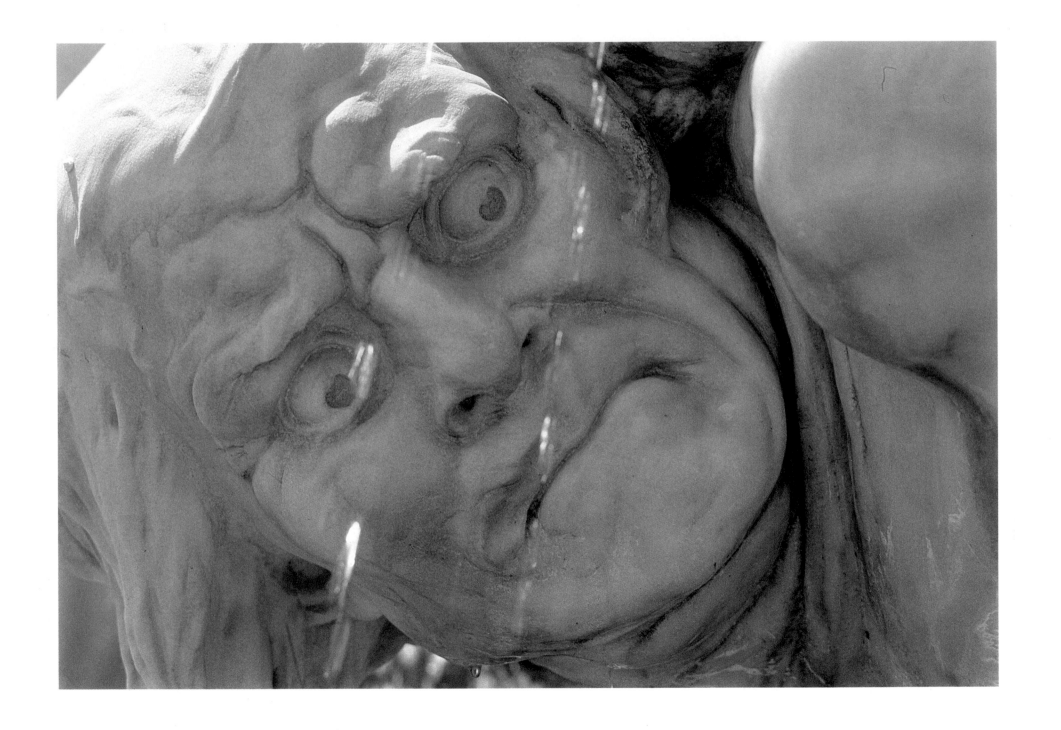

122

104 In the eyes of the musical establishment, the Vienna State Opera is the heart of Austrian national culture.
Construction of the court opera began in 1861, and the house opened on 25th May 1869 with Mozart's "Don Juan". Along with Milan's La Scala and the New York Metropolitan, it is today one of the most famous opera houses in the world. Gustav Mahler, Richard Strauss, Clemens Krauss, Wilhelm Furtwängler, Karl Böhm and Herbert von Karajan have conducted, and leading singers have given and still give guest performances here.

The architects of the opera house, Eduard van der Null and August Siccard von Siccardsburg, designed the building using various Renaissance styles. In doing so, they created a work which represents the culmination of the early Ringstrasse style.

The unique appearance of the main façade lies in the projecting loggia, the arches of which hold bronze statues by Julius Hähnel. The walls inside the loggia were decorated with scenes from Mozart's "Magic Flute" by Moritz von Schwind. The highlight of the interior design of the opera house is the main staircase, with its many romantic perspectives and prolific decorative statues by Hans Gasser.

This opera house took the place of the Kärntnertor Theater (on the site of the present Hotel Sacher), and has become a visible symbol of Vienna's century-old tradition of opera. Opera has always been close to the heart of the Viennese, and the reconstruction of the State Opera after its tragic destruction in 1945 was celebrated in grand style with a performance of Beethoven's "Fidelio" on 5th November 1955.

105–108 The Vienna State Opera has also been fertile ground for leading directors from all over the world: Jean-Piere Ponnelle and Franco Zeffirelli, Otto Schenk and Götz Friedrich are just some of the stars. Here are some of the sets from Charles Gounod's opera "Faust" in the extravagant and controversial production of Ken Russell, the English director famous for his films.

109–112 Once a year, traditionally the last Thursday of the carnival season, the house on the Ring radiates in the glamour of the Opera Ball. This most fashionable of Vienna's fashionable balls, the climax of the Vienna carnival season, is celebrated with extravagant splendour and covered in detail by the local press.

The event is arranged by a charming countess, whom the Austrian state engages specially for the occasion, and whole plane loads of flowers are flown in from the Riviera to decorate the boxes. Music is provided by the Viennese Opera Ball Orchestra, an ensemble devoted to the cultivation of specifically Viennese dance music, and other well known bands and groups. The ceremonial opening of the festivities follows a precise routine: grand fanfares, national anthem as the head of state enters his box, dances by a ball committee of young ladies and gentlemen trained in the strict rites of the ballroom – the young ladies in long white dresses, flowers in their hands and tiaras in their hair, the young men in tailcoats or uniform. This is followed by a feast for the eyes: performances by the State Opera ballet, usually of Strauss waltzes. The ceremonial of court festivities seems to live on in this exciting event.

Distinguished ball-goers from all over the world hurry to Vienna to share the fun with the members of the Austrian government, the diplomatic corps, prominent personalities from economic and cultural life and the élite of local singers and actors.

113–117 The fiacre: a popular Viennese attraction, particularly with tourists. The name "fiacre" comes from the "rue de fiacre" in Paris, where hackney carriages once had their stand.

These horse-drawn carriages – known to the Viennese as "zeugl" – have existed in Vienna since the end of the 17th century. Their once considerable number has dwindled to barely three dozen today. You can find fiacres on specific stands, such as in front of St. Stephan's Cathedral, on Heldenplatz and in front of the Albertina by the opera. From there you can be driven through the picturesque streets of the inner city or along the Ringstrasse. On the way the drivers, who have always had a reputation for being eccentric characters full of coarse bearishness, but also good natured and humorous, explain the sights in broad Viennese dialect. Some of them still wear the traditional pepita trousers and a velvet jacket, but the mark of all of them is a stiff, usually black hat.

118 A grim face looks down from the enormous wall fountain by the entrance to the Hofburg on Michaelerplatz. There are two wall fountains on the façade of the Michael wing of the Hofburg: on the west front of the gateway is "Power on Land", created in 1897 by Edmund Hellmer, and on the east front "Power at Sea", completed by Rudolf Weyr in 1895.

The Michael wing of the Hofburg was erected by Ferdinand Kirschner in 1889–1893 to amended plans by Joseph Emanuel Fischer von Erlach.

119 The whole city is transformed into a stage and exhibition hall during the Festival of Vienna – a great cultural event and popular spectacle which takes place in early summer. The artist Christa Müller, for example, populated the inner city of Vienna with dolls.

People's unexpected encounters with dolls as a medium brought the relationship between dolls and humans up for discussion. Here a larger-than-life veiled doll beside an original Viennese.

120–125 The pedestrian precinct in the inner city includes Vienna's most elegant shopping streets – Kärntner Strasse, Graben and Kohlmarkt – and is filled with pulsating, colourful life day and night. It provides an attraction for both Viennese and

tourists alike, particularly for young people. Exclusive, and correspondingly expensive shops and boutiques invite you to stroll, look and buy, cafés and restaurants spill in southern style onto the streets, and everywhere crowds of curious onlookers gather around young artists, singers and musicians. The inner city of Vienna is in, and its interesting bistros and wine bars make it a popular meeting-place for a more or less alternative young society.

126 The monument to the eminent Austrian poet Franz Grillparzer in the Volksgarten. Grillparzer was the creator of modern psychological drama, and is referred to by the Viennese as the third German classical writer. The larger-than-life seated marble figure of the poet was created by Carl Kundmann, while the architectural design was the work of Karl Hasenauer. The reliefs by Rudolf Weyr on the architecturally elaborated wall behind the monument depict scenes from Grillparzer's dramas.

127–129 The flea market held every Saturday on Wienzeile near the Naschmarkt will make notalgic hearts beat a little faster. Under mountains of old clothes and absolute junk you can still find the odd curious and unusual item, dolls and art nouveau lamps with faded silk lampshades, yellowing books, wind-up

gramophones and much more besides. Haggling over a purchase adds to the fun: jokes are cracked and Viennese humour is given free rein. Although in recent years an increasing number of professional second-hand dealers have mixed in with the stall holders, the flea market is still worth a visit, especially in view of its entertaining atmosphere.

130·131 On Shrove Tuesday people have recently taken to wearing colourful masks in Vienna too, although the many balls and fancy-dress parties are more typical of the Vienna carnival. In the ball calendar you will find such a multitude of entertainments of all kinds that you could go to up to a dozen different events every evening.

132 Billiard players in the tradition-steeped Café Sperl on Gumpendorfer Strasse. This café is L-shaped as the famous Ringstrasse cafés once were. Plush, chandeliers and crystal glass impart an atmosphere of nostagic contentment.

Vienna's coffee-houses are islands of comfort where you can spend happy hours quietly reading newspapers and periodicals, writing letters, articles, or even entire books, talking with friends or doing business, playing chess, cards or billiards – and of course drinking coffee in all its many variations. One is not at home, and yet still not in the fresh air, as Alfred Polgar once wrote.

133 The "k. u. k. Hofzuckerbäckerei Ch. Demel's Söhne": this patisserie is a relic of the imperial age and the sweetest of all addresses in a city renowned for its delicious cakes and pastries.

Demel's on Kohlmarkt near the Hofburg was once the meeting-place of the aristocracy and Vienna's high society. Although from time to time the shop still has prominent customers today, wafting of exquisite lavender water, the little marble tables are usually surrounded by tourists out to enjoy the flair of a world that once was great and apparently hale. However, the quality of the sweet delicacies has remained unchanged since the establishment was founded in 1776. The croissants, Danish pastries, strudels, gugelhupfs, cakes, sweetmeats, etc. are still prepared to secret old recipes. But even the savoury specialities, such as crab salad or paté, reveal the master's touch.

Another vestige of the imperial age is the dignified polite manner of the waitresses, who, dressed in shiny black, address the customer in formal German phrases.

The Viennese cabaret artistes Gerhard Bronner and Helmut Qualtinger have poked fun at this old Viennese institution where nostalgia has become a trade mark in their "chorus of Demel waitresses":

"We are the very last defendresses
Of a genuine Viennese tradition,
And we act like the ancient priestesses
Of an almost forgotten religion."

134–139 The Prater – that unique combination of extensive parklands with ancient trees, alleys, meadows and pools, of sports arena and amusement park – is still a great attraction for both Viennese and tourists, both young and old. It is not just the children who enjoy the Prater fun-fair with its maze of amusements, such as roundabouts, roller coasters, ghost trains, halls of mirrors, shooting ranges and slot machines, with its popular restaurants, cafés and variety shows.

One of the main attractions is the "Riesenrad" – a giant Ferris wheel which, with a few interruptions in times of trouble, has been turning since 1897. Rising to a height of 67 metres, the cabins offer a magnificent view of the Prater and the city and its surroundings. The Ferris wheel – at the time a marvel of modern engineering – was erected by the English designer Walter Basset and his fellow engineer Hitchins. After being severely damaged during the war, this landmark of Vienna and symbol of the will to survive was renovated in 1947 and has since proved to be a lasting sensation.

140–145 Vienna's horse-racing centres are also to be found in the extensive grounds of the Prater. Gallop races are held at Freudenau, where there was a jousting field in the second half of the 14th century and a fashionable racecourse was built in 1868, and at Krieau there is a trotting course. As in other large cities, horse-races also play an important role in Viennese society, and they are a meeting place for elegant folk, an opportunity to see and to be seen.

146 The whole world is present via radio and television when the Vienna Philharmonic Orchestra gives its famous New Year's concert in the great hall of the Musikverein. The concert is entirely devoted to the "Strausses", the family of musicians who dominated the musical life of Vienna for two generations and whose fame is immortal. The great hall with its gilded caryatids adds to the festive mood of the concert: this is the show-piece of the Musikverein building which Theophil Hansen built in 1867–1870 for the Society of the Friends of Music founded in 1812. When the exhilarating strains of the Blue Danube waltz – known as Austria's "national anthem" – by Johann Strauss the younger are heard at the end of the concert, and when finally the stirring Radetzky March by Johann Strauss the elder is conducted full of enthusiasm by the conductor, violin in hand as Johann Strauss himself once did, the house explodes in raptures of joy.

On the outskirts of the metropolis

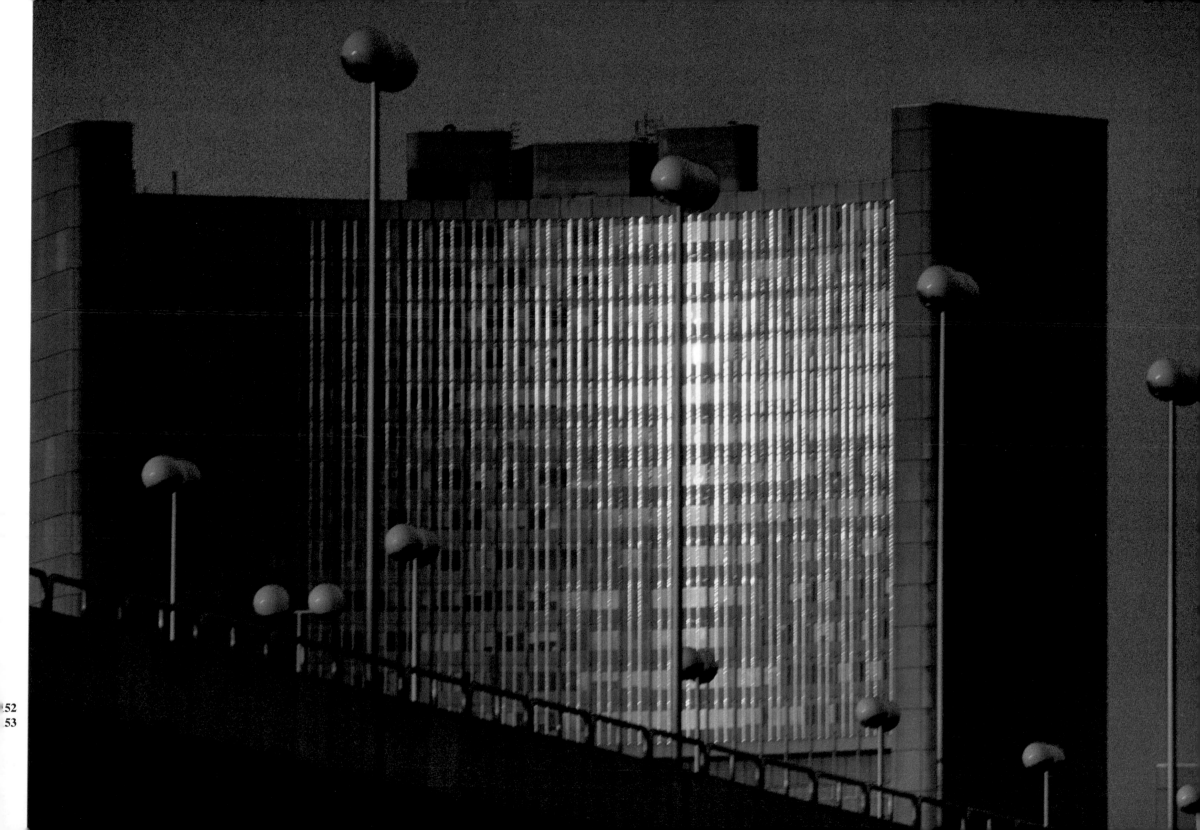

17.
17.

47 A trip to Kahlenberg, especially on days with clear visibility, is one of the unforgettable experiences of a visit to Vienna. From here, where the Polish king Sobieski mustered his relieving army to go to the aid of the sorely pressed Viennese during the siege by the Turks, one has a magnificent panoramic view of the city. The Danube tower, soaring 252 metres into the night sky, is one of the "new" landmarks of Vienna.

48 The "Danube Island", now the last Danube regulation project to relieve the river of floodwater, has almost been completed. The view from Nestroy Bridge extends over several Danube bridges to Kahlenberg.

49 The pleasure steamer "Theodor Körner" by Nestroy Bridge (Theodor Körner was mayor of Vienna after 1945 and subsequently president of the Second Republic). The two-tier bridge erected after the collapse of the "Reich Bridge" was named after Johann Nestroy not least due to his play "Below Stairs and Upstairs".

50 The headquarters of the Danube Steam Shipping Company, established in 1829, are located on Handelskai. It is from here that steamers leave on regular Danube trips to well known destinations such as the Wachau, Melk Abbey and neighbouring Hungary.

151·153 Cosmopolitan blends with suburban on the left bank of the Danube – in "Transdanubia". This is also the location of the Vienna International Center, the United Nations headquarters (architect Johann Staber). The significance of Vienna as a congress venue and the headquarters of the I.A.E.O. and U.N.I.D.O. has been consolidated by the construction of an adjoining congress centre.

152 The houseboats of the fishermen along the Danube are still fairly numerous and impart a touch of nostalgia. In their spare time, the fishermen catch fish in nets in accordance with ancient tradition.

154 In Schwechat, a town on the outskirts of Vienna, is the ÖMV oil refinery. Crude oil produced in Austria and also that pumped up the Adriatic pipeline from the Mediterranean and former imperial harbour of Trieste is processed at the refinery to produce fuels and other high quality petrochemical products.

155 Vienna's international airport – also located at Schwechat – is an important centre of national, European and international air traffic and is used by many airlines. This is due not least to "Austrian Airlines", the national airline, with its international distinctions.

156·157 An outstanding blend of existing buildings and modern architecture can be found in many places in Vienna. This is illustrated by the successful construction of an administration building for the Creditanstalt Bankverein (CA), Austria's largest bank, on the site of Franz Josef train station.

158 In an effort to make municipal housing more flexible and attractive, the City of Vienna has initiated "Austrian Artists Build for the Viennese", a large-scale project which has been acclaimed throughout Europe.
Friedensreich Hundertwasser, internationally renowned graphic artist and painter by profession, made a start with this house in Löwengasse.

159 By way of contrast, one of the first large-scale "social housing" projects, the "Karl Marx Hof". Built in 1930 to plans by Karl Ehn, it was certainly the most spectacular and modern council housing complex of its time. A three-storey front extends over a distance of 1.2 kilometres, and it is remarkable that each of the 1,600 odd flats has its own loggia looking out onto one of the enormous green courtyards.

160 This "lighthouse of peace" by the Danube, the first pagoda on the European continent, was consecrated in 1983 by monks of the Buddhist Nipponzan Myohoji order.

161 The Orient begins in Vienna. An amusing expression becomes reality. In 1979 the Islamic Center erected a mosque with a 32 metre high minaret amidst the allotment gardens not far from the United Nations headquarters.

162 Generally referred to as the "Wotruba Church", the "Church of the Holy Trinity" was erected on Georgenberg in the Vienna district of Mauer in the years 1974–1976 to plans by the prominent Austrian sculptor Fritz Wotruba. He constructed his church, whose silhouette stands out bizarrely against the sky, of massive concrete blocks which give the whole church a slightly megalithic appearance.

163·164 Wolfgang Amadeus Mozart died alone and in poverty in Vienna in 1791. This world famous Austrian, who was acclaimed as a child in Maria Theresa's time and highly celebrated in later life, found his last resting place in a pauper's grave in St. Marx Cemetery.

165·166 Named after its "inventor", a Leipzig doctor who did a great deal for public health, gymnastic training and the establishment of public playgrounds for children, the "Schreber" garden is still an oasis of relaxation and recreation in our day. Council land within the city limits is divided into plots to give people in and around Vienna a pleasant environment in their own little house and garden.

167 The Danube at Vienna was regulated in 1871–1875, the arms of the river being combined together. Only the southern arm of the Danube, the Danube Canal, actually flows through the middle of Vienna, while the main bed of the river touches the city on the periphery. After regulation of the river, the remains of an arm remained as the "Alte Donau", a recreational area for the Viennese.

168 Ten minutes by underground train from Stephansplatz, the flood relief channel stretches on either side of the "Donau-insel" underground station. Here on the "Viennese Riviera", a seemingly endless beach where nudists are naturally also tolerated, both young and old alike plunge into the refreshing, clean water to recover from the heat and commotion of the big city.

169–172 The heuriger and Vienna: two concepts apparently inseparably connected with one another. The "heuriger" is both a wine tavern and last year's wine, which is served at such establishments.
The wine which grows around Vienna has been greatly appreciated ever since Roman times. The emperor Probus is reputed to have introduced wine-growing to this region.
The "heuriger" came into being with a decree issued by Emperor Joseph II in 1784 legally regulating the sale of self-grown wine. The wine-growers hung up their green sprigs of pine, originally a sign for the tax collector.
The heuriger had its heyday during the Biedermeier age. Thus we know of excursions to the heurigers which Franz Schubert undertook with his friends, accompanied by the music of the popular "Strauss" and "Lanner". For a hundred years now, "Schrammel" music has gladdened the hearts and minds of heuriger visitors.
The vineyards of the wine-growers cover a part of the country which Beethoven was familiar with, but Nussdorf, Sievering and Neustift are also well known wine-growing villages.

173–179 The Vienna Woods cover some of the last foothills of the Alps, with flourishing vineyards and dense beech woods in the north and black pine trees in the south. The landscape is made up of gently rolling hills and wide fertile meadows.
It should not be taken for granted that this untouched landscape has been preserved for us on the outskirts of the city. Time and time again, this wonderful recreation area for hikers and nature lovers in the immediate vicinity of Vienna has been and is threatened with destruction. About a hundred years ago, for example, the Vienna Woods were saved from imminent deforestation by speculators at the initiative of the local Mödling politician Josef Schöffel.
Today the dangers come from a different source: they are the civilisational diseases of our age.

Thoughts on photography

Pictures rule our lives, overcoming all linguistic and ideological barriers, and have developed into the most important information medium of the 20th century.

For each of us, this means being inundated with stimuli, but at the same time sensitises us to the medium itself. Today photography is certainly met with a new understanding. Apart from pure documentation, our interest is perceptibly shifting from mere observation to the desire to see and create independently. Thus to an increasing extent photography serves to capture our personal, irretrievable impressions.

Individual illustrated volumes are an important part of this new way of thinking. They are a kind of school for the sight and help an interested observer to a new picture of the environment.

There are many sides to Vienna.

For this reason, the one hundred and eighty-two photographs in this volume certainly take the observer to a Vienna seen completely subjectively. Much is missing, while other things in turn are over complete.

Any claim to completeness has given way to that of an "unconventional, different point of view", although the basic goal of showing "beautiful Vienna" was pursued. The collection of pictures grew alongside many other jobs over a period of about three years. Many obstacles had to be overcome on the way. Whereas on the one hand renovation work obstructed the view of the cathedral, the door to many other motives was opened only thanks to the support of well disposed benefactors. To them, and to all those who had a hand in the realisation of this project, I should like to say: "Thank you".

I should just like to add the following remarks about the following photographic details for the enthusiastic photographer:

Photography is painting with light. For me the most important creative criterion in colour photography is consciously using the available light and the resulting colouring.

For this reason, I used no filters, with the exception of a polarising filter. Many of the photographs were taken with a tripod if this was allowed or possible. In exceptional cases I also held the camera by hand even for lengthy exposures (up to 1 second with a wide-angle lens). My favourite film material is still the 64 ASA slide film, as it reproduces my perception of colour best. For this reason, in bad light conditions I would rather use a high-power objective than a highly sensitive film. Thus only very few photographs were made on 400 ASA film; I used the 160 ASA artificial light film for indoor photographs without daylight.

In keeping with the trend of the times, I have recently started using the Minolta Autofocus SLR system in addition to my conventional Minolta reflex equipment.

Hans Wiesenhofer

Photographic details